Managing Trauma Workbook for Teens

A TOOLBOX of REPRODUCIBLE ASSESSMENTS and ACTIVITIES for Facilitators

Ester R.A. Leutenberg
and John J. Liptak, EdD

Duluth, Minnesota

101 W. 2nd St., Suite 203
Duluth, MN 55802

800-247-6789

books@wholeperson.com
www.wholeperson.com

Managing Trauma Workbook for Teens
A Toolbox of Reproducible Assessments and Activities
for Facilitators.

Copyright ©2015 by Ester R.A. Leutenberg and John J. Liptak.
All rights reserved. Except for short excerpts for review purposes
and materials in the activities and handouts sections, no part of this
workbook may be reproduced or transmitted in any form by any
means, electronic or mechanical without permission in writing from
the publisher. Activities and handouts are meant to be photocopied.

All efforts have been made to ensure accuracy of the information
contained in this book as of the date published.

The author(s) and the publisher expressly disclaim responsibility
for any adverse effects arising from the use or application of the
information contained herein.

Printed in the United States of America

10 9 8 7 6 5 4 3 2 1

Editorial Director: Carlene Sippola
Art Director: Joy Morgan Dey
Assistant Art Director: Mathew Pawlak

Library of Congress Control Number: 2015908642
ISBN: 978-157025-335-5

Introduction

Managing Trauma Workbook for Teens

When people think about and talk about the experience of trauma, there is a tendency to associate the condition with adults, however, trauma is also experienced by children and teens. For many children who experience trauma, reactions and problems do not manifest themselves until adolescence or adulthood.

For teens, the symptoms related to a traumatic event are much the same as those for adults. Effects and reactions to trauma are significant and stressful. Teens who go through a personal event involving trauma, or who are exposed to an overwhelmingly stressful event or series of events, will continue to emotionally and physically re-experience the event and suffer from it repeatedly, possibly for a long time.

Trauma can be life-changing. The activities in the *Managing Trauma Workbook for Teens* can be a tremendous benefit to any teenager who has experienced stress from a traumatic episode.

People perceive many types of events as stressful and feel that stress as a result of having experienced them; however they are too numerous and too individualized to describe.

See below for some of the causes of trauma:

- Abandonment
- Abuse
- Almost drowning
- Attack by animals
- Attack by a person
- Attempted or witnessed suicide
- Blackmail
- Bombing
- Bystander of bullying
- Car or plane crash
- Changes within the family
- Child/teen abuse
- Chronic disease or illness
- Criminal assault
- Cult activities
- Dangerous weather conditions
- Explosion
- Falling
- Fire
- Harassment by peers or adults
- Illegal issues
- Incest
- Injury
- Kidnapping

- Loss of a body part
- Loss of the use of a body part
- Mugging
- Natural disaster
- Neglect
- Observing abuse
- Physical proximity to a tragedy
- Rape
- Riots
- Robbery
- Seeing the death of someone
- Sexual abuse
- Sudden life-threatening illness
- Terrorist attack
- Threat to safety
- Threatened with a weapon
- Torture
- School shootings
- Suicidal pacts
- Victim of bulling
- Violence
- Witness to a crime
- Witnessed anything terrible
- Others

How Does Trauma Manifest Itself?

All teens experience some type of stress, but not all teens suffer the severe disruptive stress reactions associated with traumatic events. The difference between the experience of traumatic events and regular, ordinary stressful events depends on an individual's perception of the events and the person's individualized reactions. Each person's experience is valid and treatable. For some teens, the symptoms of trauma dissipate after several months, yet some symptoms can continue to recur for years, or forever.

Because there are so many ways stress from a traumatic event can manifest itself, symptoms can be very difficult to identify and manage. It is critical to be aware of, and to understand, how symptoms are commonly experienced. Although most or all symptoms do not have to be present, those that are present will typically cause significant distress and/or impairment in a person's daily functioning.

Some symptoms that interfere with the daily functioning of teens:

- Experiencing upsetting memories of the event that interfere with daily functioning
- Avoiding people and places that are reminders of the event
- Becoming angry at negative feedback
- Changing personality abruptly
- Diminishing relationships with peers
- Engaging in impulsive and risky behavior
- Engaging in out-of-place sexual behavior
- Exhibiting outbursts of anger
- Experiencing an abrupt change in personality
- Experiencing appetite changes
- Experiencing concentration, focus and memory problems
- Experiencing high levels of anxiety
- Experiencing nightmares related to the event
- Failing grades and other academic problems
- Failing to develop positive relationships with peers and adults
- Failing to fall or stay asleep
- Feeling detached from others
- Feeling emotionally numb, or avoiding thoughts and feelings that are reminders
- Feeling fatigued a lot of the time
- Feeling irritable
- Feeling jumpy and easily startled
- Feeling pain/distress when remembering the event
- Having an attitude: "I hate you" or "You can't make me"
- Having flashbacks and feelings that the event is happening again
- Lacking motivation
- Losing interest in activities that at one time were pleasurable
- Losing interest in life
- Making unlikely decisions
- Manipulating
- Not controlling reactions
- Remembering, or not, important aspects of the trauma
- Sensing that a future once imagined is no longer attainable
- Skipping school – truancy
- Starting to abuse unhealthy substances
- Unusually poor relationship with teachers
- Zoning out for long periods of time

Losing interest in life and in activities that were once pleasurable, plus some of the above and additional symptoms, may relate to traumatic events and/or other mental health issues.

Introduction

INFORMATION FOR FACILITATORS
When Using the Managing Trauma Workbook for Teens

Our main goal for this workbook is NOT to diagnose a mental illness, or expect the facilitator to make that diagnosis from this workbook's content. Our goal is to touch on some of the symptoms and possibilities, create realizations, and provide coping methods which will help people to go forward and perhaps consider the possibility of the need for consideration of medications and therapy.

Our secondary goal is also to help teens recognize that other people have the same issues, that no shame is connected to them, and that mental health issues of any degree are not to be stigmatized nor should anyone need to feel like a victim of stereotyping. In this workbook, we use the phrase mental health issues in order to include ALL types of trauma symptoms and problems, from just losing one's temper to indicators of a serious mental illness.

Seek Professional Help!

Teens who experience severe bouts of trauma-related symptoms may need to seek professional help from a medical or psychological professional. Some of the questions you can evaluate to determine if professional assistance is needed:
- Has the teen been experiencing these symptoms for a longer time than usual, lasting perhaps for weeks or even months?
- Are these trauma symptoms causing bigger problems at school, at a salaried or a volunteer job, at home, or in the teen's community?
- Have the person's efforts to manage the symptoms of trauma failed?
- Does the person feel hopeless and helpless in trying to change problematic symptoms after experiencing a trauma?

Teens need to do much more than complete the assessments, activities and exercises contained in this workbook if they have serious mental issues. All trauma-related symptoms and problems need to be thoroughly evaluated by a medical professional and then treated with an appropriate combination of medication and group and/or individual therapy.

CONFIDENTIALITY

Instruct teens to use NAME CODES when writing or speaking about anyone. Teens completing the activities in this workbook might be asked to respond to assessment items and journal about relationships. Before you begin using the materials in this workbook explain to teens that confidentiality is a term for any action that preserves the privacy of other people. Maintaining confidentiality is extremely important, for it shows respect for others and allows – even encourages - teens to explore their feelings without hurting anyone's feelings or fearing gossip, harm or retribution.

In order to maintain this confidentiality, ask teens to assign a NAME CODE for each person they write about as they complete the various activities in the workbook. For example, **a friend named Pat** who **Loves To Sing** might have the code name of **LTS** for a particular exercise. In order to protect their friends' identities, they will not use people's actual names or initials, just NAME CODES.

Managing Trauma Workbook for Teens

Some Teen Reactions to a Trauma

- Constant talk about the traumatic event.
- Demonstrate increased impulsive and/or rebellious behaviors.
- Display self-absorption.
- Experiences difficulties with short-term memory, focusing, concentration and problem solving.
- Feels emotions such as depression, sadness, anger, anxiety, hopelessness, and/or guilt.
- Give up responsibilities.
- Harbors feelings of hopelessness.
- Has a pessimistic outlook on life.
- Have disturbed sleeping patterns.
- Isolate from people and events.
- Lash out with excessive aggression, and violence.
- Lose interest in school, friends, and life.
- Need independence.
- Overreact to minor irritations.
- React by out-of-the-ordinary sexual behavior.
- Refusal to talk about the traumatic event. Keeping it all inside.
- Repetitively think about the traumatic event.
- Self-harm in attempts to experience and express feelings.
- Show protective behavior of family and friends.
- Turn to substances as a means of escape.
- Withdraw from family and friends.

Helping Teens Cope with Reactions to a Trauma

Teens who have survived trauma display complex sets of symptoms that need to be addressed if they are to heal. Following are some of the ways that facilitators can assist their clients to process traumatic events, learn to manage the symptoms of trauma, and begin the transition to a more satisfied life.

- Help participants learn as much as possible about reactions to trauma.
- Help participants explore their traumatic event in a structured, safe way. Consult a mental health professional to decide if the process will be therapeutic for an individual.
- Help participants accept their traumatic events and the impact these events have on their lives while focusing on the importance of taking actions to cope with their reactions to traumatic stress.
- Help participants see the importance of being proactive in coping with the stress associated with their traumatic events.
- Help participants understand that recovery from traumatic events will not happen immediately, but will happen a little at a time.
- Help participants accept that the purpose may not necessarily be to forget their traumatic events, but rather to accept what happened and learn to cope with the issues they are experiencing.
- Help participants understand and develop a plan for recognizing and coping with both the physical, emotional, psychological and interpersonal symptoms that they are experiencing.
- Help participants learn to identify the triggers that bring on reactions to their traumatic stress, and learn to cope with these triggers.
- Help participants learn skills for making the transition to a more manageable and satisfying life.

Introduction

How the *Managing Trauma Workbook for Teens* Can Help

Teens who have experienced a traumatic event are likely to develop a variety of symptoms associated with that event. The assessments and activities in this workbook are designed to provide facilitators with a wide variety of tools to use in helping teens manage their lives more effectively. Many choices for self-exploration are provided for facilitators to determine which tools best suit the unique needs of their clients.

The purpose of this workbook is to provide a user-friendly guide to short-term assessments and activities to help teens manage their issues related to trauma and to experience a greater sense of well-being. In addition, this workbook is designed to provide facilitators and participants with tools and information needed to overcome the stigma attached to the reactions of trauma issues.

In order to help participants successfully deal with reactions to traumatic events, facilitators need to have a variety of assessments and activities to help their participants open-up and begin to manage the symptoms of traumatic issues. The *Managing Trauma Workbook for Teens* provides assessments and self-guided activities to help participants understand the intensity of their issues and how they can establish ways to lead a more effective life.

When to Worry?

The symptoms related to traumatic events can be very complex and difficult to cope with. The good news is that teens can develop symptom management skills and progress toward more satisfying lives. The symptoms that accompany traumatic event issues that teens deal with daily can be very frightening. Teens who experience this over time are at risk of having serious mental issues. Participants who have serious mental issues need to do much more than complete the assessments, activities and exercises contained in this workbook. They need to be taken seriously. Facilitators can take an active role in their finding help immediately. All disturbances of thoughts, feelings and actions need to be thoroughly evaluated by a medical professional, and then treated with an appropriate combination of medication and group and/or individual therapy.

Suicide Warning!

Many trauma survivors have suicidal thoughts and make plans to die by suicide. Sometimes they think that the only way to escape the physical, psychological, and emotional pain is to attempt suicide. Remember to take any talk about suicide or suicidal acts very seriously.

Some Signs of Suicidal Thoughts:

- Withdrawing from family, friends, and activities of interest in the past
- Increasing use of harmful substances
- Giving away possessions
- Expressing severe hopelessness about the future
- Making a plan for dying by suicide
- Calling or visiting people to say goodbye
- Getting affairs in order
- Engaging in reckless actions
- Talking about killing or harming self
- Expressing feelings of being trapped with no way out
- Purchasing a weapon

Format of the *Managing Trauma Workbook for Teens*

The *Managing Trauma Workbook for Teens* is designed to be used either independently or as part of an established mental health issue program. You may administer any of the assessments and the guided self-exploration activities to an individual or a group with whom you are working, and you may administer any of the assessments and activities over one or more days. Feel free to pick and choose those that best fit the outcomes you desire. The purpose of this workbook is to provide facilitators who work with individuals and groups who may be experiencing issues related to traumatic events with a series of user-friendly reproducible activities to supplement their work with participants. Because these activity pages are reproducible, they can be photocopied as is, or you may adapt them by whiting out and writing in your own changes to suit the need of each group, using that page as your master to be photocopied for each participant.

Assessments
Assessments establish a behavioral baseline from which facilitators and participants can gauge progress toward identified goals. This workbook will supplement the facilitator's work by providing assessments designed to measure behavioral baselines for evaluating client change. In order to do so, assessments with scoring directions and interpretation materials begin each module. The authors recommend that you begin presenting each topic by asking participants to complete the assessment. Facilitators can choose one or more, or all of the activities relevant to their participants' specific needs and concerns.

Each of the awareness modules contained in this book begin with an assessment for these purposes:
- Help facilitators to develop a numerical baseline of behavior, attitude and personality characteristics before they begin their plan of treatment.
- Help facilitators gather valuable information about their participants.
- Help facilitators in the measurement of change over time.
- Use as pre-tests and post-tests to measure changes in behavior, attitude, and personality.
- Help facilitators identify patterns that are negatively affecting a participant.
- Prompt insight and behavioral change.
- Assist participants to feel a part of the treatment-planning process.
- Provide participants with a starting point to begin to learn more about themselves and their strengths and limitations.

Assessments are a great aid in developing plans for effective change. Be aware of the following when administering, scoring, and interpreting the assessments in this workbook:
- The purpose of these assessments is not to pigeonhole teens, but to allow them to explore various elements of themselves and their situations.
- This book contains self-assessments and not tests. Traditional tests measure knowledge or right or wrong responses. For the assessments provided in this workbook, remind participants that there are no right or wrong answers. These assessments ask only for opinions or attitudes.
- The assessments in this workbook have face value, but have not been formally normed for validity and reliability.
- The assessments in this workbook are based on self-reported data. In other words, the accuracy and usefulness of the information is dependent on the information that participants honestly provide about themselves. Assure them that they do not need to share their information with anyone. They can be honest!
- Remind participants that the assessments are exploratory exercises and not a judgment of who they are as human beings.
- The assessments are not a substitute for professional assistance. If you feel any of your participants need more assistance than you can provide, refer them to an appropriate medical professional.

(Format continued on the next page)

Introduction

Format of the *Managing Trauma Workbook for Teens* (Continued)

Assessment Script

When administering the assessments contained in this workbook, please remember that the assessments can be administered, scored, and interpreted by the client. If working in a group, facilitators should circulate among participants as they complete assessments to ensure that there are no questions. If working with an individual client, facilitators can use the instruction collaboratively.

Please note that as your participants begin the assessments in this workbook, the participants' instructions italicized below are meant to be a guide, so please do not feel you must read or say them word for word.

Tell your participants: *"You will be completing a quick assessment related to the topics we are discussing. Please remember that assessments are powerful tools if you are honest with yourself. Take your time and be truthful in your responses so that your results are an honest reflection of you. Your level of commitment in completing the assessments honestly will determine how much you learn about yourself."*

Allow participants to turn to the first page of their assessment and read the instructions silently to themselves. Then tell them: *"All of the assessments have similar formats, but they have different scales, responses, scoring instructions and methods for interpretation. If you do not understand how to complete the assessment, ask me before you turn the page to begin."*

Then tell them: *"Because there is no time limit for completing the assessments, take your time and work at your own pace. Do not answer the assessments as you think others would like you to answer them or how you think others see you. These assessments are for you to reflect on your life and explore some of the barriers that are keeping you from living a more satisfying life. Before completing each assessment, be sure to read the instructions."*

Make sure that nobody has a question, then explain, *"Learning about yourself can be a positive and motivating experience. Don't stress about taking the assessments or discovering your results. Just respond honestly and learn as much about yourself as you can."*

Tell participants to turn the page and begin answering with Question 1. Allow sufficient time for all participants to complete the assessment. Answer any questions people have. As people begin to finish, read through the instructions for scoring the assessment. Have participants begin to score their own assessment and transfer their scores for interpretation. Make sure that nobody has a question about how to do the scoring.

Review the purpose of the interpretation table included after each assessment. Tell the participants: *"Remember, this assessment was not designed to label you. Rather, it was designed to develop a baseline of your behaviors. Regardless of how you score on an assessment, consider it a starting point upon which you can develop healthier habits. Take your time, reflect on your results, and note how they compare to what you already know about yourself."*

After participants have completed, scored, and interpreted the assessment, facilitators can use the self-exploration activities included in each module to supplement their traditional tools and techniques to help participants function more effectively.

(Continued on the next page)

Format of the *Managing Trauma Workbook for Teens* (Continued)

Self-Exploration Activities

This workbook will provide self-exploration activities that can be used to help manage trauma issues. These activities, included after each of the assessments, will prompt self-reflection and promote self-understanding. They use a variety of formats to accommodate all learning styles, foster introspection, and promote pro-social behaviors, life skills and coping skills. The activities in each module correlate to the assessments to enable you to identify and select activities quickly and easily.

Self-exploration activities assist participants in self-reflection, enhance self-knowledge, identify potential ineffective behaviors, and teach more effective ways of coping with irrational behaviors. They are designed to help participants make a series of discoveries that lead to increased social and emotional competencies, as well as to serve as an energizing way to help participants grow personally and to learn important life skills. These brief, easy-to-use self-reflection tools are designed to promote insight and self-growth.

Many different types of guided self-exploration activities are provided for you to pick and choose the activities that are most needed by your participants and the ones that will be most appealing to them. The unique features of the exploration activities make them user-friendly and appropriate for a variety of individual sessions and group sessions.

In these activities, participants will have a variety of opportunities:
- To explore how they could make changes in their lives to feel better. These activities are designed to help participants reflect on their current life situations, discover new ways of living more effectively, and implement changes in their lives to accommodate these changes.

- To journal as a way of enhancing their self-awareness. Through journaling prompts, participants will be able to write about the thoughts, attitudes, feelings, and behaviors that have contributed to, or are currently contributing to, their current life situation. Through journaling, participants are able to safely address their concerns, hopes and dreams for the future.

- To explore their reactions to trauma by examining their past for negative patterns and learning new ways of dealing more effectively in the future. These activities are designed to help participants reflect on their lives in ways that will allow them to develop healthier lifestyles.

Introduction

The Stigma Awareness Approach

It is important that facilitators keep an open mind about mental health issues and the stigma attached to people experiencing these issues. Rather than thinking of people as having a mental disorder, or being mentally ill, the *Erasing the Stigma of Mental Health Issues through Awareness* series is designed to help facilitators to diminish the stigma that surrounds people who are experiencing reactions to traumatic events. Stigmas occur when people are unduly labeled, which sets the stage for discrimination and humiliation. Facilitators are able to help to erase the stigma of mental illness through enhanced awareness of the factors that activate the issues, accentuate the depth of the issues, and accelerate awareness and understanding.

To assist you, a section titled *Erasing the Stigma of Mental Health Issues* is included to provide activities for helping to erase the stigma associated with reactions to trauma issues.

The Awareness Modules

The reproducible awareness modules contained in this workbook will help you identify and select assessments and activities easily and quickly:

Module I: My Trauma Story
This module will help teens share all aspects of their story in a safe way and put it into a positive perspective.

Module II: My Escape-ism
This module will help teens explore the various ways that they avoid and numb themselves to forget their traumatic experience, and provides tools for coping with these symptoms.

Module III: My Transition
This module will help teens explore ways that they can effectively manage trauma and move on from their traumatic experience.

Module IV: Tools for Coping
This module will help teens explore the various ways that they re-experience their trauma and provides tools for coping with these symptoms.

Module V: Erasing the Stigma of Mental Health Issues
This module will help teens explore the stigma of having experienced a traumatic event in their lives and the impact that the stigma has on them.

Our thanks to these professionals who make us look good and who personify people who are dedicated to erasing the stigma of mental health issues.

Art Director – Joy Dey
Assistant Art Director – Mathew Pawlak
Editorial Director – Carlene Sippola

Editor: Eileen Regen, M.ED., CJE – Lifelong Teacher
Reviewer: Carol Butler, MS Ed, RN, C – Skills Expert
Reviewer: Nadine Hartig, Ph.D., LPC, LCSW – Trauma Counselor
Reviewer: Beth Jennings, CTEC – School Counselor
Reviewer: Niki Tilicki, MAED – School Teacher and Counselor
Reviewer: Jay Leutenberg, CASA – Proofreader Extraordinaire

Table of Contents

MODULE I – MY TRAUMA STORY 17
Skills Emphasized in Each Activity Handout. 18
My Trauma Story Scale Introduction and Directions. 19
My Trauma Story Scale. 20
Scoring Directions. 21
Profile Interpretation 21
Scale Descriptions. 21
My Trauma Story 22
Thoughts About My Trauma 23
Me – Before My Trauma. 28
What I Was Like Before My Trauma 29
Who I Am Now 30
My View of the World 31

MODULE II – MY ESCAPE-ISM 33
Skills Emphasized in Each Activity Handout. 34
My Escape-ism Scale Introduction and Directions 35
My Escape-ism Scale 36
Scoring Directions. 37
Profile Interpretation 37
Scale Descriptions. 37
Avoiding Places 38
Avoiding People. 39
Avoiding Situations 40
Suppressing My Feelings 41
Feeling My Feelings 42
Avoiding My Feelings?. 43
Avoiding Situations 40
Picturing My Fear. 44
I Feel Guilty!. 45
Who Created the Trauma? 46
Expressing Feelings 47
Escaping through Addiction 48
Ways I Shut Down 49
Zoning Out 50
Ways I Self-Harm 51
Alternatives to Self-Harm 52

Table of Contents

MODULE III – MY TRANSITION 53
Skills Emphasized in Each Activity Handout 54
My Transition Scale Introduction and Directions 55
My Transition Scale 56
Scoring Directions 57
Profile Interpretation 57
Scale Descriptions 57
Close Relationships 58
Connected or Not 59
Trust 60
My View of Others 61
Physical Boundaries 62
My Safety Plan 63
Physical Safety 64
Environmental Safety 65
Emotional Safety 66
A Safety Contract 67
My Safe Places 68
Victim Thinking 69
A Historical Perspective 70
Why am I So Angry? 71
My Angry Moments 72
Constructive Vs. Destructive Anger Management 73
Mandala 74
Hopefulness 75
Self-Esteem 76
My Strengths and My Talents 77
Re-Writing Your Narrative 78
Solving My Problem 79
My Wish 80
Add Life Structure 81

Managing Trauma Workbook for Teens

Table of Contents

MODULE IV – MY COPING TOOLS 83
    Skills Emphasized in Each Activity Handout........................... 84
    My Coping Tools Scale Introduction and Directions 85
    My Coping Tools Scale 86
    Scoring Directions... 87
    Profile Interpretation 87
    Scale Description.. 87
    Intrusive Thoughts 88
    My Trauma Triggers.. 89
    Trigger Management 90
    My Nightmare and My Trauma 91
    The Value of Positive Distractions 92
    Flashbacks 93
    My Sleep Patterns 94
    Tracking My Sleep Patterns 95
    Sleep Tips 96
    Jittery, Anxious? Edgy? Jumpy? Agitated?
        Worried? Scared? Skittish? 97
    Over-Cautious?.. 98
    Problem Solving for the Overly-Cautious 99
    Anticipating High-Risk Situations 100
    Coping: Let's Meditate.. 101
    Coping: Deep Breathing 102
    Coping: Mindfulness and Paying Attention 103
    Coping: Total-Body Relaxation 104
    Ways to Make Meaning 105

Introduction

Table of Contents

MODULE V – ERASING THE STIGMA OF MENTAL HEALTH ISSUES 107
Skills Emphasized in Each Activity Handout 108
Erasing the Stigma of Mental Health Issues Introduction 109
Two Types of Mental Health Stigma 110
The Stigma of Trauma – THE PAST 111
The Stigma of Trauma – THE PRESENT 112
Speak Your Mind 113
If We Stamp Out the Stigma 114
Glenn Close said 115
Effects of Trauma Issues 116
The Stigma of Going to a Mental Health Therapist 117
Stereotypes 118
Will You Speak Out? 119
My Negative Thoughts 120
Focus on Your Strengths 121
Ways I Try to Minimize My Trauma Stress 122
Ways I am Treated 123
Self-Doubt 124
A Poster about the STIGMA of People Who
    Have Experienced a Trauma 125
A Poster about ACCEPTANCE of People Who
    Have Experienced a Trauma 126
DE-STIGMA-TIZE with the Facts about Mental Health Issues 127
Coping with the Stigma of a Mental Health Issue 128
Speak Out Against Stigmas 129

MODULE I

My Trauma Story

There is no greater agony than bearing an untold story inside of you.

~ Maya Angelou

Name _____

Date _____

Managing Trauma Workbook for Teens

Skills Emphasized in Each Activity Handout

My Trauma Story ....page 22
   Journal details and feelings about the trauma.

Thoughts About My Trauma ....page 23
   Respond to 17 prompts to help make meaning of the trauma and reduce stress.

Me – Before My Trauma ....page 28
   Show self-identity specifics by depicting and describing self before the trauma.
   Identify aspects of identity that seem to be missing since the traumatic event.

What I Was Like Before My Trauma ....page 29
   Describe personal traits before the trauma by responding to five questions.

Who I Am Now ....page 30
   Describe personal traits after the trauma by responding to five questions.

My View of the World ....page 31
   Share personal views of the world by completing five sentences-starters.

My Trauma Story Scale
Introduction and Directions

If you have experienced a traumatic event, it is important to explore what you have experienced in an atmosphere of feeling safe, not re-experiencing the trauma or feeling overwhelmed. Therefore it is important to tell your story safely and begin to integrate aspects of your traumatic event into your overall identity. To begin to tell and understand your story, it will help to explore your experience, self-identity and trauma triggers.

This assessment contains 18 statements designed to help you explore the various aspects that surround your trauma story. Read each of the statements and decide whether the statement describes you or not. If the statement does describe you, circle the number in the YES column next to that item. If the statement does not describe you, circle the number in the NO column next to that item. Do not worry about the numbers for now.

In the following example, the circled 2 indicates the statement does describe the person completing the scale:

ABOUT MY TRAUMA EVENT	YES	NO
I have shared the story of my trauma with my family and friends	2	1

This is not a test. Since there are no right or wrong answers, do not spend too much time thinking about your answers. Be sure to respond to every statement.

(Turn to the next page and begin.)

My Trauma Story Scale

ABOUT MY TRAUMA EVENT…	YES	NO
I have shared the story of my trauma with my family and friends	2	1
I often think about what happened to me	2	1
I understand how the traumatic event has had an impact on me	2	1
I can't make sense of why it had to happen	1	2
I become upset all over again when I re-experience the event	1	2
I don't want to think about the event	1	2

SCALE I = _____

ABOUT MY TRAUMA EVENT…	YES	NO
I don't recognize the person I am anymore	1	2
I still see the world as a good place	2	1
I feel guilty, ashamed and/or embarrassed about what happened	1	2
I feel good about myself even though the event happened	2	1
I have isolated myself from friends and/or family	1	2
I believe I am not a good person because of what happened	1	2

SCALE II = _____

ABOUT MY TRAUMA EVENT…	YES	NO
I have no idea of what will trigger my memories	1	2
I know how to calm down when I am reminded of the event	2	1
I never know when something will trigger the memory of the event	1	2
I have a plan for when I begin to feel stressed about the event	2	1
I know the situations that are challenging for me	2	1
Many sights and sounds trigger memories of my trauma	1	2

SCALE III = _____

(Go to the Scoring Directions.)

My Trauma Story Scale
Scoring Directions

The *My Trauma Story Scale* you just completed is designed to measure your readiness to tell your trauma story. For each of the sections on the previous page, count the scores you circled. Put that total on the line marked TOTAL at the end of each section.

Then, transfer your total to the space below:

    I = My Experience Total   TOTAL _____

    II = My Self-Identity Total   TOTAL _____

    III = My Triggers Total   TOTAL _____

Add your scores together for your GRAND TOTAL _____

Profile Interpretation

Individual Score	Grand Total	Result	Indications
6 - 7	18 - 23	Low	Low scores indicate that you have not accepted and integrated the traumatic event into your life.
8 - 10	24 - 30	Moderate	Moderate scores indicate that you have somewhat accepted and integrated the traumatic event into your life.
11 - 12	31 - 36	High	High scores indicate that you have accepted and integrated the traumatic event into your life.

Scale Description

I. **My Experience** – Teens scoring high on this scale have made sense of the trauma they experienced, shared their story to others in an open, honest and direct way, and integrated their trauma into other life experiences.

II. **My Self-Identity** – Teens scoring high on this scale have a positive view of themselves and the world in general. They do not feel guilty, ashamed or embarrassed about what happened to them and they feel good about themselves.

III. **My Triggers** – Teens scoring high on this scale are aware of their trauma triggers and have explored and integrated ways to manage these triggers in their lives.

GRAND TOTAL – High scores on all three scales indicate that the teen is aware of the impact of their trauma on their life and has made strides to integrate the traumatic event with current daily experiences. The following pages will be helpful to everyone, no matter how they scored.

Managing Trauma Workbook for Teens

My Trauma Story

Telling one's story is healing! Many people who experience trauma feel guilty, ashamed or embarrassed to tell anyone their story. A great way to tell your story safely is by writing it out.

In the space that follows, write about the trauma that you experienced in as much detail as possible. Use the back of this page if you need additional space. Use Name Codes.

Thoughts About My Trauma - PAGE 1

Think about the trauma you experienced.
Journaling about that experience can help make meaning of the event and reduce distress.

Below, journal about your trauma. Use Name Codes.

When did the event happen? _____
_____

What was happening before the event? _____
_____
_____
_____
_____
_____
_____
_____
_____

How were you feeling on the day of the trauma? (*happy, sad, normal, jittery, jumpy, worried, etc.*)
_____

Explain your feelings. _____
_____
_____
_____
_____
_____
_____
_____

(Continued on the next page)

My Trauma Story

Thoughts About My Trauma - PAGE 2

What do you remember about the event (sights, smells, sounds, feelings, thoughts)?

_____
_____
_____
_____
_____
_____
_____
_____
_____
_____
_____

How did you know it was over? _____

_____
_____
_____
_____
_____
_____
_____
_____

(Continued on the next page)

My Trauma Story

Thoughts About My Trauma - *PAGE 3*

What did you do after it was over? _____
_____
_____
_____
_____
_____
_____
_____
_____
_____
_____

In what ways has the event changed your life? _____
_____
_____
_____
_____
_____
_____
_____
_____
_____
_____

(Continued on the next page)

Thoughts About My Trauma - PAGE 4

In what ways has the event changed you?

_____
_____
_____
_____
_____
_____
_____

In what ways has the event changed your relationships with family?

_____
_____
_____
_____
_____
_____
_____

In what ways has the event changed your relationships with friends?

_____
_____
_____
_____
_____
_____
_____

(Continued on the next page)

Thoughts About My Trauma - *PAGE 5*

How have your future plans changed in a **negative** way?

How have your future plans changed in a **positive** way?

Managing Trauma Workbook for Teens

Me - Before My Trauma

Your self-identity can change as the result of a trauma.
It can help you to explore the way you were before the trauma.

In the space that follows, draw, doodle, write about or list words and phrases that describe who you were before your trauma. Use Name Codes.

What parts of your identity seem to be missing since the traumatic event?

_____

_____

What I Was Like Before My Trauma

Think about yourself before you experienced the traumatic event. What were you like?

Answer the following questions to get a more comprehensive sense of who you were.

In what were you interested before the trauma?

_____
_____
_____

What made you happy before the trauma?

_____
_____
_____

What made you sad before the trauma?

_____
_____
_____

What did you like most about yourself before the trauma?

_____
_____
_____

What were your dreams before the trauma?

_____
_____
_____

My Trauma Story

Managing Trauma Workbook for Teens

Who I Am Now

Think about yourself after you experienced a traumatic event. What are you like now?

Answer the following questions to get a more comprehensive sense of who you are now.

In what are you interested now?

_____
_____
_____

What makes you happy now?

_____
_____
_____

What makes you sad now?

_____
_____
_____

What do you like most about yourself now?

_____
_____
_____

What are your dreams now?

_____
_____
_____

My Trauma Story

My View of My World

Experiencing a trauma can definitely change the way people view the world in general.

In the space that follows, describe how you now view your world. Use Name Codes.

I believe the world is a _____ place because
_____
_____
_____

The things in this world that I care most about are _____
_____
_____
_____

The things I cannot control include _____
_____
_____
_____
_____

Through my positive actions, I can make positive changes including
_____
_____
_____
_____

My life would be better if I could _____
_____
_____
_____

MODULE II

My Escape-ism

*You will find peace,
not be trying to escape
your problems, but
by confronting them
courageously.*

~ J. Donald Walters

Name _____

Date_____

Managing Trauma Workbook for Teens

Skills Emphasized in Each Activity Handout

Avoiding Places...page 38
Identify four places that are avoided, the associated memories, and how one is hindered by the avoidance. Differentiate between the easiest and most difficult to avoid, and state the reasons.

Avoiding People...page 39
Identify four people that are avoided, the associated memories, and how one is hindered by the avoidance. Differentiate between the easiest and most difficult to avoid, and state the reasons.

Avoiding Situations...page 40
Identify four situations that are avoided, the associated memories, and how one is hindered by the avoidance. Differentiate between the easiest and most difficult to avoid, and state the reasons.

Suppressing My Feelings..page 41
Demonstrate insight into emotional numbness by completing seven sentence-starters related to feelings. Personalize a quotation about the danger of suppressing feelings and benefits of expressing feelings.

Feeling My Feelings...page 42
Select and/or add the personally most descriptive terms or facets of four basic emotions. State which are felt the most, when, and where the feelings occur.

Avoiding My Feelings?..page 43
Identify five or more ways one avoids feelings, what is avoided, and the effects. State one or more reasons for the avoidance and give one example.

Picturing My Fear...page 44
Sketch a picture or caricature of a personal fear or panic attack. Then draw how one would like the fear to appear. State ways to reduce the fear.

I Feel Guilty!..page 45
Rate the intensity of personal guilt on a ten-point scale. Demonstrate insight by responding to five questions about a personal role in the traumatic event.

Who Created the Trauma?...page 46
Identify four people who contributed to or created the trauma. Share how one was hurt, and feelings toward the people. Identify personal steps to let go of the negative feelings and/or forgive.

Expressing Feelings...page 47
Express eight negative emotions and their positive counterparts by completing fourteen insight-oriented sentence-starters.

Escaping through Addiction..page 48
Identify five ways one may numb oneself through addictive behaviors, and their detrimental effects of each. Document five or more healthy alternatives. State the addictive behavior one most wants to stop and steps to take to do so.

Ways I Shut Down..page 49
Identify personal ways of shutting down by responding to six or more prompts. Describe the negative and positive effects on self and relationships. State ways to stop shutting down.

Zoning Out...page 50
Elaborate about nine or more avoidance activities and the time spent on them. Describe nine or more helthy alternative diversions.

Ways I Self-Harm...page 51
Select which self-harm actions are personally used from among ten possibilities. Rank the personal top three self-harmful behaviors and state when they are used.

Alternatives to Self-Harm..page 52
Depict positive ways to feel alive and healthy, and productive alternatives to self-harm by creating a photo gallery of drawings, doodles, magazine pictures and other images.

My Escape-ism Scale
Introduction and Directions

Teens who have experienced a traumatic event attempt to protect themselves from the intense emotions involved in the event by escaping: avoiding, becoming emotionally numb, and tuning out of the present.

Many teens will attempt to avoid dealing with their traumatic experience by trying to avoid everything associated with the event, including the following:
- Avoiding people, places and situations
- Numbing by emotionally escaping the present situation

This assessment contains 30 statements designed to help you explore how much you try to avoid dealing with the trauma you experienced. Choose your most traumatic situation and briefly write it on the line at the top of the page. Read each of the statements and decide whether the statement describes you or not. If the statement does describe you, circle the number in the YES column next to that item. If the statement does not describe you, circle the number in the NO column next to that item.

In the following example, the circled 2 indicates the statement does describe the person completing the inventory:

	YES	NO
I try to ignore my memories and hope they'll go away	(2)	1

This is not a test. Since there are no right or wrong answers, do not spend too much time thinking about your answers. Be sure to respond to every statement.

(Turn to the next page and begin.)

Managing Trauma Workbook for Teens

My Escape-ism Scale

My Traumatic Situation _____

	YES	NO
I try to ignore my memories and hope they'll go away	2	1
I have turned my back on the event	2	1
I can't face the trauma	2	1
It hurts too much to handle the memories	2	1
I want the memories to go away	2	1
I avoid anything that reminds me of the trauma	2	1
I avoid places that remind me of the trauma	2	1
I avoid people that remind me of the trauma	2	1
I don't want to recall details of the trauma	2	1
I don't leave the house for fear of similar situations	2	1
I cannot talk with anyone who was part of the trauma	2	1
I feel guilty about the event and avoid discussing it	2	1
I avoid talking with anyone who asks me about it	2	1
I use substances to avoid my thoughts	2	1
I use my addiction to avoid my thoughts	2	1

I. Total = _____

	YES	NO
I have shut my feelings down	2	1
I'm afraid of being overwhelmed by my feelings	2	1
I can't feel anything	2	1
I feel embarrassed about the event	2	1
I don't want to feel anything	2	1
I feel separated from others	2	1
I often find it difficult to concentrate	2	1
I harm myself to feel alive	2	1
I isolate myself	2	1
I act like a robot without feelings	2	1
I daydream a lot to escape life	2	1
I want to sleep a lot to escape my life	2	1
I often feel separate from my body	2	1
I only remember certain aspects of my trauma	2	1
I feel numb in certain situations	2	1

II. Total = _____

(Go to the Scoring Directions.)

My Escape-ism Scale
Scoring Directions

The *My Escape-ism Scale* you just completed is designed to measure how much you attempt to avoid remembering your traumatic experience, and how you numb yourself and your feelings. For both of the sections on the previous page, count the scores you circled. Put that total on the line marked TOTAL at the end of each section. Then, transfer your total to the space below:

    I   =   Avoiding   TOTAL _____
    II   =   Numbing   TOTAL _____

    Add your scores together for your GRAND TOTAL _____

Profile Interpretation

Individual Score	Grand Total	Result	Indications
15 - 19	30 - 39	Low	Low scores indicate that you do not seem to avoid and numb your symptoms.
20 - 25	40 - 51	Moderate	Moderate scores indicate that you sometimes seem to avoid and numb your symptoms.
26 - 30	52 - 60	High	High scores indicate that you often seem to avoid and numb your symptoms.

Scale Description

Avoiding – Teens scoring high on this scale tend to ignore their trauma, and ultimately avoid people, places, and situations that are reminders.

Numbing – Teens scoring high on this scale attempt to numb themselves with the use of illegal substances, harming themselves and daydreaming, as well as being unable to deal with their feelings effectively.

GRAND TOTAL – High scores on both scales indicate that the person uses numbing and avoiding as a way of not dealing with intrusive memories, flashbacks, and feelings associated with having experienced a trauma. The following activities will be helpful to everyone, no matter how they scored.

Avoiding Places

Teens often want to forget and stop re-experiencing their traumatic event. This is a natural reaction If that is true of you, you are probably spending a lot of your life avoiding places that remind you of the trauma.

Answer the following questions to identify how much effort you are exerting to avoid the places that would bring back memories of your trauma.

A Place I Avoid	What This Place Reminds Me of	What I Miss by Avoiding This Place
EXAMPLE: Going to the park.	The setting of my traumatic event.	I loved to take my dog for walks there.

Which places are the easiest to avoid?

Why is it easy to avoid these places?

When is it most difficult? Why?

My Escape-ism

Avoiding People

Teens often want to forget and stop re-experiencing their traumatic event. This is a natural reaction. If that is true of you, you are probably spending a lot of your life avoiding people that remind you of the trauma.

Answer the following questions to identify how much effort you are exerting to avoid the people that would bring back memories of your trauma. Use Name Codes.

A Person I Avoid	What This Person Reminds Me Of	What I Miss by Avoiding This Person
EXAMPLE: SLK	She reminds me of my mother, who neglected me.	I miss not going over to my friend's house as much as I want to.

Which people are the easiest to avoid?

How do you avoid them?

Which are the most difficult?

Why?

Managing Trauma Workbook for Teens

Avoiding Situations

Teens often want to forget and stop re-experiencing their traumatic event. This is a natural reaction. If that is true of you, you are probably spending a lot of your life avoiding situations that remind you of the trauma.

Answer the following questions to identify how much effort you are exerting to avoid the situations that would bring back memories of your trauma. Use Name Codes.

A Situation I Avoid	What This Situation Reminds Me Of	What I Miss by Avoiding This Situation
EXAMPLE: Going on dates without other trusted people present.	One of my best friends was drugged and raped while on a date. It was terrible!	I don't think I can even hold hands let alone be intimate with anyone. That makes me sad.

Which situations are the easiest to avoid?

How do you avoid them?

Which situation is the most difficult?

Why?

My Escape-ism

Suppressing My Feelings

Sometimes it is easier for those who have had traumatic events in their life to simply try to suppress their feelings so that they don't have to feel them anymore; they become emotionally numb.

For the following activity, answer each of the sentence starters below.

Feelings I would rather hide include …

The feelings I have and enjoy include …

The feelings I am no longer able to feel include …

The feelings I think I no longer deserve to feel include …

The feelings I am embarrassed to feel include …

The feelings I am ashamed to feel include …

The feelings I do not feel safe expressing include …

> *We all know that being able to express deep emotion can literally save a person's life, and suppressing emotion can kill you both spiritually and physically.*
> ~ Lisa Kleypas

In the box above, read, and then cross out "We all" and write "I."
Cross out "a person's" and write "my." Cross out "you" and write "me."
Then read the quotation to yourself.

Feeling My Feelings

Teens who have experienced a trauma often try to avoid their feelings. An important strategy is to identify the emotions you feel. Below are four basic feelings with many facets of each feeling.

Look at the listings of feelings and add your own to identify which degree of the emotion you feel most. Use Name Codes.

You Become Angry – Annoyed, Bitter, Furious, Outraged, Hostile, Enraged, Mad
Which of these do you feel the most? When do you experience the feeling? Where are you?

_____

_____

_____

You Feel Glad – Caring, Calm, Relaxed, Content, Fulfilled, Delighted, Loved, Peaceful
Which of these do you feel the most? When do you experience the feeling? Where are you?

_____

_____

_____

You are Sad – Helpless, Pessimistic, Useless, Depressed, Miserable, Hurt, Disappointed
Which of these do you feel the most? When do you experience the feeling? Where are you?

_____

_____

_____

You Become Scared – Vulnerable, Terrified, Devastated, Fearful, Victimized, Frantic
Which of these do you feel the most? When do you experience the feeling? Where are you?

_____

_____

_____

My Escape-ism

Avoiding My Feelings?

Teens who have experienced very painful emotions try to control their pain by shutting off their emotions.

Think about how you avoid your feelings, what you avoid and the effects this avoidance has on you. Use Name Codes.

Ways I Avoid My Feelings	What I Avoid	The Effect this Has on Me
Example: *I stay away from places that might trigger feelings.*	*I avoid athletic events that remind me of the traumatic event.*	*I enjoy sports and I miss out on supporting our team.*
I stay away from places that might trigger feelings.		
I stay away from people who might trigger feelings.		
I try not to think of memories that bring back my feelings.		
I try to stay numb.		
I am not comfortable feeling any emotions.		
Other		

Why do you think you avoid your feelings? Give an example. _____

_____

_____

Managing Trauma Workbook for Teens

Picturing My Fear

Many teens feel afraid after they have experienced a trauma. Some may have panic attacks.

One way to gain control over your fear and/or panic is to use your imagination and draw a picture or a caricature of what your fear and/or panic attack looks like to you.

\[drawing box\]

Is the picture as fearful as you think it is? How can you reduce your fearful feelings?

_____

_____

_____

On the other side of the page, draw what you'd like your fear or panic to look like.

My Escape-ism

I Feel Guilty!

Guilt occurs when you feel responsible after something traumatic has happened, whether you were an active participant or not. Even though you may not have had a part in the trauma you experienced (or even if you did), you may feel guilty after a traumatic event.

Answer the questions below to explore your level of guilt. Use Name Codes.

My level of guilt about what happened to me (place an X on the line below):

0--10
Not Guilty   **Very Guilty**

What was the traumatic event?

_____
_____
_____

What do you feel guilty about?

_____
_____
_____

Why did you choose to handle the situation as you did?

_____
_____
_____

What would you do differently?

_____
_____
_____

How realistic is your guilt? Explain

_____
_____
_____

Who Created the Trauma?

It is important to explore the feelings you have about the creator of the trauma that has become an issue to you.

In the table that follows identify those people who you believe created, or helped to create, your trauma(s). This may be one person or several people; someone whose name you know or do not know; a country; a leader; a group. Use Name Codes.

My Trauma _____

People Who Have Created the Trauma	How These People Hurt Me	Feelings about Those People
Example: JWB – He abused me.	He stole my faith and trust in people.	Hate, fear, sadness.
Example: TCS who brought a weapon to school and threatened to use it.	It scared me so much I don't want to go back to school.	I hate him for causing the rest of us to be so traumatized.

What steps can you take to let go of your negative feelings and/or forgive?
(That does not necessarily mean *forget*.)

_____

_____

_____

My Escape-ism

Expressing Feelings

Some teens are unable to express feelings because they are unable to find words to describe their feelings. When you are able to express positive and negative feelings, you will find that you become more content with your own feelings and can experience them more easily.

Finish the following sentence starters. If mentioning a person, use name codes.

I'm very sad about	I feel good about
I am very frightened about	I feel safe when
I feel defeated when	I feel uplifted when
I feel anxious when	I am calm when
I feel very uncomfortable when	I am comfortable when
I feel hopeless when	I feel hopeful when
I am optimistic when	I am pessimistic when
(other) I …	(other) I …

Managing Trauma Workbook for Teens

Escaping through Addictions

Some Teens, in an attempt to numb themselves from the traumatic event they experienced, use stimulants and substances, and indulge in addictive behaviors *(gambling, sexting, social media, caffeine, drugs, shopping, stealing, spending money, etc.)*.

In the spaces that follow, identify the various substances and addictive behaviors that you use to numb yourself. If you are mentioning a person, use name codes.

My Substances and/or Addictions	How this Numbs Me	How this Negatively Affects My Life	What I Could do Instead
Example: Smoking	*It distracts me. I look forward to it. I do not think about my trauma at all.*	*I have to keep borrowing money from friends to support my smoking habit.*	*I could join the baseball team again. It will distract me and I provide me with a support system.*

Which of the substances or addictive behaviors that you use to numb yourself would you like to stop the most?

_____

_____

_____

What steps can you take to stop using or doing this altogether? _____

_____

_____

My Escape-ism

Ways I Shut Down

Trauma survivors will do what they can to avoid being in situations and relationships that might trigger the traumatic event. They shut down or numb themselves.

Think about the ways you do this in your life. If you mention a person use name codes.

Ways I Shut Down	How this Affects Me and/or My Relationships in a POSITIVE Way	How this Affects Me and/or My Relationships in a NEGATIVE Way
Retreat from life		
Detach from people		
Stare off into space		
Act on autopilot		
Separate my mind from my body		
Feel apathetic		
Other		

What makes me shut down?

How can I learn to stop?

Managing Trauma Workbook for Teens

Zoning Out

Trauma survivors often find ways to protect themselves from traumatic events by *zoning out* to avoid thinking about the event. Some zoning out is healthy – too much is not!

What are some of the ways that you zone out too much, to avoid thinking about the trauma you have experienced?

Ways I Zone Out	Length of Time I Do This	What I Believe This Does for Me	Is it Healthy for Me or Not? Why?
Watch television			
Daydream			
Go to a fantasy world			
Use social media			
Play video games			
Participate in high-risk activities			
Abuse substances and/or develop addictions			
Read a spell-binding book			
Go out with friends			
Other			
Other			

My Escape-ism

Ways I Self-Harm

Many Teens who have experienced trauma in their lives will attempt to express their feelings by harming themselves.

Which of the following do you do to harm yourself? Place a check in the box in front of those that apply to you, and describe what you do. If you mention a person use name codes. You do not need to share this page. Be honest with yourself!

☐ I over-eat
_____

☐ I take excessive risks
_____

☐ I cut, burn, etc., myself
_____

☐ I use alcohol to excess
_____

☐ I smoke
_____

☐ I spend money excessively
_____

☐ I put myself in risky situations
_____

☐ I use illegal substances to excess
_____

☐ I remain in a harmful relationship
_____

☐ I have an addiction
_____

Rank your top three self-harmful behaviors and when you use them:

1) _____
2) _____
3) _____

Alternatives to Self-Harm

Teens often harm themselves to feel alive.

Prepare a collage of alternatives to self-harm *(funny movie, a hobby or craft, a therapist, a supportive person, etc.)* **that you will consider using.** This collage can include pictures cut out of a newspaper or magazine, drawings, doodles, or images from an online photo collection.

MODULE III

My Transition

A lot of people resist transition and therefore never allow themselves to enjoy who they are.

~ **Nikki Giovanni**

Name _____

Date _____

Managing Trauma Workbook for Teens

Skills Emphasized in Each Activity Handout

Close Relationships .... page 58
Demonstrate insight about six aspects of close relationships by completing sentence starters.

Connected or Not? .... page 59
Identify people with whom one does/does not feel connected, and the reasons.

Trust .... page 60
Describe how trust affects the ability to talk about and deal with trauma.

My View of Others .... page 61
Depict and/or describe significant others. State whom one wants to tell about the event.

Physical Boundaries .... page 62
Acknowledge six aspects of personal boundaries by responding to questions.

My Safety Plan .... page 63
Document a safety plan: people who can help, how, and ways to reach them. Identify safeguards.

Physical Safety .... page 64
State ways to improve safety in five specified places, plus other locales.

Environmental Safety .... page 65
Describe ways to implement each of five safety suggestions.

Emotional Safety .... page 66
List five trustworthy people one avoids, and ways to re-establish the relationships.

A Safety Contract .... page 67
Contract in writing for safety about four types of self-harm, and seeking help.

My Safe Places .... page 68
Describe four safe places, reasons, the most treasured, and why.

Victim Thinking .... page 69
Reveal signs of victim thinking; replace with nine positive affirmations.

A Historical Perspective .... page 70
State ways to adopt five aspects of an admired historical person's wisdom.

Why am I so Angry? .... page 71
Identify possible reasons for anger by responding to seven thought-provoking questions.

My Angry Moments .... page 72
Describe how anger could have been better expressed in four situations.

Constructive Vs. Destructive Anger Management .... page 73
Document and compare four or more constructive and destructive personal expressions of anger.

Mandala .... page 74
Experience a deep sense of calm and well-being.

Hopefulness .... page 75
Demonstrate hope by completing six sentences. Personalize a quotation.

Self-Esteem .... page 76
Describe one's positive traits: personality, talents, knowledge, and gifts.

My Strengths and Talents .... page 77
Identify five personal strengths, and how the trauma helps one to handle life.

Re-Writing Your Narrative .... page 78
Describe the trauma with self as hero/heroine. Share what was learned.

Solving My Problems .... page 79
Perform ten or more problem-solving steps concerning a personal difficulty.

My Wish .... page 80
Describe five aspects of one's life purpose by responding to sentence-starters.

Add Life Structure .... page 81
Document ways to reduce a personal primary trigger plus six triggers in other areas of life.

My Transition Scale
Introduction and Directions

Experiencing a traumatic event can, and probably has, changed you in a variety of ways. It is important that you accept what has happened to you, integrate the experience into your life, look to the future, and seek growth and opportunities.

This self-assessment contains 24 statements designed to help you explore how ready you are to make a transition to a better future. Read each item carefully and decide how much the statement describes you. In each of the choices listed, circle the number of your response.

In the following example, the circled number under 1 indicates the statement is **True** for the person completing the inventory.

	TRUE	FALSE
I no longer feel close to some members of my family	1	2

This is not a test and there are no right or wrong answers. Do not spend too much time thinking about your answers. Your initial response will be the most true for you. Be sure to respond to every statement.

(Turn to the next page and begin.)

My Transition Scale

	TRUE	FALSE
I no longer feel close to some members of my family	1	2
I want to have healthy friendships	2	1
I avoid getting too close to others	1	2
I still appreciate some people	2	1
I don't care about friendships anymore	1	2
I don't feel as if I can trust anyone again	1	2

SCALE 1 = _____

	TRUE	FALSE
I don't feel safe	1	2
I have a safety plan	2	1
I feel as if someone might harm me	1	2
I am careful about my situation	2	1
I am afraid I will harm myself	1	2
I am able to solve problems	2	1

SCALE 2 = _____

	TRUE	FALSE
I have lost interest in life	1	2
I can see a happy future for myself	2	1
I feel hopeless	1	2
I am too stressed about my trauma to enjoy life	1	2
I feel like I can't control my future	1	2
I know many good things will happen in my life	2	1

SCALE 3 = _____

	TRUE	FALSE
I can control my feelings	2	1
I have angry outbursts	1	2
I become upset easily	1	2
I know techniques for managing my anger	2	1
I often have moments of rage	1	2
I say things out of anger that I am sorry for later	1	2

SCALE 4 = _____

(Go to the Scoring Directions.)

My Transition Scale
Scoring Directions

The My Transition Scale is designed to help you explore how ready you are to move on and make the transition to a new life. On the self-assessment page, add the numbers that you circled in each section and write the scores on each of the TOTAL lines. You will receive a total in the range from 6 to 12. Then, transfer those numbers to the space below.

Scale 1	=	Positive Relationships	TOTAL _____
Scale 2	=	Feeling Safe	TOTAL _____
Scale 3	=	Overcoming Hopelessness	TOTAL _____
Scale 4	=	Managing Anger	TOTAL _____

Profile Interpretation

Individual Score	Result	Indications
6 - 7	Low	If you scored in the LOW range, you are not ready to move on from the traumatic event you experienced.
8 - 10	Moderate	If you scored in the MODERATE range, you are fairly ready to move on from the traumatic event you experienced.
11 - 12	High	If you scored in the HIGH range, you are ready to move on from the traumatic event you experienced.

Scale Description

Positive Relationships – Teens scoring high on this scale still care about people, trust others, and want to have intimate relationships in their lives.

Feeling Safe – Teens scoring high on this scale have a safety plan in place, are not a threat to harm themselves, and do not fear others.

Overcoming Hopelessness – Teens scoring high on this scale are interested in life, expect positive things to happen to them, and plan to have a great future.

Managing Anger – Teens scoring high on this scale are able to control their emotions, especially angry outbursts.

Close Relationships

In order to move on from traumatic events it is important to maintain close relationships with supportive people in your life. Often, teens who have experienced a trauma find it difficult to develop and maintain close relationships.

If any of these sentence starters do not apply to you, explain. Use Name Codes.

I am uncomfortable talking about myself because …

Since my trauma I've not been able to get close to …

I must know people well before I can trust them because …

I've had a difficult time being in a dating relationship because …

My friends don't understand me because…

My trauma has affected my home life …

//My Transition

Connected or Not?

Closeness to others illustrates your ability to feel truly connected to other people.
For a variety of reasons, you may be feeling disconnected to important people in your life.

**Complete the tables below to explore the level of your relationships with others.
Use Name Codes.**

People I FEEL Connected To and the Level of this Relationship	How and Why I FEEL Connected
EXAMPLE: CHR – We've been close for years.	*I was able to confide in her about my trauma because I knew that she would support me.*

People I DO NOT FEEL Connected To and the Level of this Relationship	Why I DO NOT Feel Connected and Do I want to Improve It?
EXAMPLE: JLP – We haven't gotten along since the trauma.	*He feels like I am trying to draw attention to myself. He tells me to "move on." I am in a group to deal with my trauma and he has agreed to come with me to some meetings. I think this will improve our relationship as he is able to understand.*

Which table was easier to complete? _____

Why? _____

_____

Trust

For a variety of reasons, you may be having a hard time trusting other people.
Being able to trust another person means feeling safe and secure in your relationship with this person.
Think about those you trust and those you do not trust.

Complete the table that follows to explore those people you TRUST. Use Name Codes.

People I trust	Why I trust this person	Have I talked to this person about my traumatic event? Why or why not?
EX. KLS	She's always been there for me, no matter what.	Yes, and she's been accepting and non-judgmental.

Complete the table that follows to explore those people you CANNOT TRUST.

People I do not trust	Why I do not trust them	Ways this affects my ability to deal with the traumatic event
EX: GLS	We used to be so close but recently he told other relatives that I'm to blame.	I don't have another male to talk with but he doesn't try to understand me or my situation.

Which table was easier to complete? _____

Why? _____

_____

_____

My Transition

My View of Others

Many teens feel differently about people in their lives after having experienced a trauma. How do you view important others in your life?

You can use sentences to describe these people, draw what you think they look like, or write one-word descriptors. Use Name Codes.

With whom would you like to share about what happened to you? _____
_____
_____
_____

What or who can help you do that? _____
_____
_____

Physical Boundaries

If you have experienced a trauma in your life, you possibly have, or will set up, physical boundaries that you keep with various people in your life. A physical boundary is the amount of space you feel that you need around you when interacting with other people.

Answer the following questions to explore your physical boundaries. Use Name Codes.

The amount of space I need between me and other people to feel comfortable and safe is
_____

Is this boundary the same for all people? If not, for whom is it different and why?
_____
_____
_____

How do you maintain your physical boundary?
_____
_____
_____

How do you feel when someone crosses your physical boundary?
_____
_____
_____

How do you react when this happens?
_____
_____
_____

How do you tell others if you feel like they are crossing your physical boundary?
_____
_____

My Transition

My Safety Plan

Everybody has the right to feel safe in their daily lives. Safety is the feeling of freedom from harm inflicted by you or other people. Whether you feel the need to talk to someone, or go to a safe place, there are people who can help ensure that you are safe.

In the spaces that follow, identify those people who can help you and how they can help you. In the third column, list the best method to reach each person. Use Name Codes.

People Who Can Help	How This Person Can Help	How I Can Contact This Person
EXAMPLE: My friend SJP	She is a great listener.	I can send her a text message.

Some tips for staying safe:

Which do you do? Place an X in the boxes of the items you are already doing. Add your own.

☐ Check the locks on the doors and windows of your home.
☐ Take a self-defense class.
☐ Have an escape plan if you need one.
☐ Be aware of your environment.
☐ Avoid risky places.
☐ _____
☐ _____
☐ _____

Physical Safety

You need to feel physically safe and protected from harm if you are going to be able to move past the trauma you experienced. As you stay physically safe, you will remain in the present, feel grounded, and feel competent to make positive life decisions.

Think about the places where you either feel safe or do not feel safe. Use Name Codes.

Places	Why I Feel Safe or Unsafe in this Place	How I Can Feel Safe or Safer in this Place
Home		
Work		
Community		
School		
Place of Worship		
Other		
Other		

My Transition

Environmental Safety

You have the right to live your life free from harm from other people.

Following are some of the ways that you can develop greater environmental safety:

Remove yourself or avoid people who are harming you or who might harm you.

How can you do this?

_____

_____

_____

Know who will help you and how they can help you.

Who are these people and how can they help you?

_____

_____

_____

Develop an emergency escape plan.

How can you do this?

_____

_____

_____

Ensure you are living in a safe place.

How can you do this?

_____

_____

_____

Be aware of your environment and avoid going into risky places alone.

How can you do this?

_____

_____

_____

Managing Trauma Workbook for Teens

Emotional Safety

People who are moving on from a traumatic event do not isolate themselves from other people. They are interested in reconnecting with people in their lives, and making new friends.

Who are the trustworthy people from whom you have isolated yourself, and what can be done to re-establish your relationships with these people? Use Name Codes.

People I Feel Isolated From	Why I Feel This Way	What I Can do to Re-establish This
EXAMPLE: JML	*He does not understand how I feel.*	*I can try to talk openly with him and help him to better understand what happened to me.*

Which relationship do you want to re-establish the most? Why?

_____

_____

My Transition

A Safety Contract

By filling in the blanks on this contract, you will agree to live the rest of your life safely and in a way that will not induce self-harm. Complete the following contract and sign and date it. Keep it handy so that you can see it daily. **Use Name Codes.**

I, _____, agree to the following:
NAME

I WILL not try to escape the pain of my trauma by (example: mutilate my body by _____, harm others, use these illegal substances _____, risk _____, etc.	I WILL manage the pain of my trauma by… (example: remain positive, continue going to school, talk to trusted people like _____, etc.

I agree to seek professional help if I _____

_____   _____
NAME   DATE

© 2015 WHOLE PERSON ASSOCIATES, 101 W. 2ND ST., SUITE 203, DULUTH MN 55802 • 800-247-6789

Managing Trauma Workbook for Teens

My Safe Places

One thing you can do to feel safe is to identify or create safe places. In thinking of your safe place, it should be where you and nobody else can access. In this place you feel safe and secure.

In the spaces that follow, write about or draw four of your favorite safe places, and describe what allows you to feel safe in each of them.

Safe Place 1	**Safe Place 2**
Safe Place 3	**Safe Place 4**

Which of these four is the safe place that you treasure the most, and why?

_____

_____

If you are not near your safe place, what does it take to make any place feel safe for you?

_____

_____

My Transition

Victim Thinking

Victim thinking is a fearful, negative view of the life, one's self and the world as a result of living through a traumatic event.

The following checklist will allow you to explore how much you use victim thinking. For each of the items that follow, place a check mark in the boxes that apply to you and then write why you think those statements are true.

- ☐ I believe I can never be loved again. _____
- ☐ I have no control over the bad things that are going to happen. _____
- ☐ I am afraid of the future. _____
- ☐ Things will never get better for me. _____
- ☐ I must be extra good to compete with other people. _____
- ☐ I will always feel traumatized. _____
- ☐ I will never be as good as other people. _____
- ☐ I can never succeed. _____
- ☐ I feel different from other people. _____
- ☐ I cannot make my life any better than it is. _____
- ☐ I feel like I need to apologize a lot. _____
- ☐ I am unworthy. _____
- ☐ I am afraid what happened to me might happen again. _____
- ☐ I feel misunderstood. _____
- ☐ I am negative most of the time. _____
- ☐ I wish the event had never happened. _____
- ☐ I will never trust again. _____

Affirmations

Following are some of the affirmations you can say to yourself to feel less like a victim.
Cut them out and put them in places where you can see them (wallet, mirror, computer)

I refuse to be a victim!	I am lovable!	I am better every day!
I can overcome!	I can reach out when I need to!	My life matters!
I am cared about!	I am special!	I WILL PUT THIS BEHIND ME!
I AM IMPORTANT!	I make a difference!	I'm worth it!

Managing Trauma Workbook for Teens

A Historical Perspective

Think about a historical figure whom you have always admired. This person could be a politician, artist, writer, film star, activist, musician, or any other figure you admire.

Name your historical figure, explain why you admire this person, and then answer the following questions from this historical figure's perspective.

Who is the historical figure you admire?

Why do you admire this person?

If that person were alive, what would he or she say to you about the trauma you have been through?

What advice would this person have for you?

What would this person say about how you have handled the trauma you experienced?

How would this person suggest that you move on from the trauma?

From what you just wrote, how can you integrate these insights into your life?

Why am I So Angry?

Unresolved anger is often felt by a person who has experienced a traumatic event. This anger is intensified when reminded of the event. It is important to explore why you feel angry about your traumatic event.

These questions will guide you through this process.
Think about why you feel angry at times. Use Name Codes.

Are you angry because the trauma occurred at all? Explain.

Are you angry because the trauma happened to you? Explain.

Are you angry because you did not do more? Explain.

Are you angry because someone else suffered? Explain.

Are you angry because you have not recovered? Explain.

Are you angry because you feel as if you cannot heal? Explain.

Are you angry because life just isn't fair? Explain.

My Angry Moments

All people become angry, but people who function well understand the situations in which they get angry, and then are able to effectively control their angry feelings.

What are some of the situations in which you express your anger inappropriately? Use Name Codes.

My Angry Moment Situation	Why I Become Angry	How I Expressed My Anger	How I Could Have Expressed it More Appropriately
Example: I get angry when my friends try and get me to talk about my trauma.	*I say to myself, I don't want to talk to them about it.*	*I am abrupt with them and do not want to hang out with them.*	*I could explain to them that I don't want to talk about the situation with them.*

Which angry-moment situations are negatively affecting your life the most? _____

_____

_____

_____

Constructive Vs. Destructive Anger Management

Think about some of the ways that you express anger in your life. Some of these ways are constructive and some are probably destructive and hurt people in your life.

Whether at home, at work, in school, or in the community, describe some of the ways you express anger constructively (talking to a support person, journaling your feelings, etc.), and some of the ways you express anger destructively (destroy things, abuse others physically, emotionally, verbally, sexually. etc.). Use Name Codes.

Constructive	Destructive

Compare the items in both columns and think about whether you need to work on your anger management issues.

Managing Trauma Workbook for Teens

Mandala

Mandalas are sacred circles that have been long been used to facilitate meditation. People create and look at mandalas essentially to center the body and mind. People who color mandalas often experience a deep sense of calm and well-being, and it can be remarkably soothing and nourishing. Mandalas not only focus your attention, but allow you to express your creative side.

Color the following Mandala however you like, or create your own.

My Transition

Hopefulness

Teens who enjoy a low level of stress and a feeling of general well-being have hopes and dreams for the future.

Explore your hopes for the future in the spaces that follow.

I hope I can …

I hope my family will …

I hope my friends will …

I hope at work I can …

I hope I don't …

I hope the people involved in my trauma …

> *Hope is being able to see that there is light despite all of the darkness.*
> *~ Desmond Tutu*

What is your light despite all of the darkness?

_____

_____

_____

Managing Trauma Workbook for Teens

Self-Esteem

The experience of a traumatic event can cause teens to question their sense of who they are. The negative effects of a trauma can be overcome by your ability to develop a positive sense of who you are as a person.

In each of the blocks that follow, cut out words from magazines, catalogues or newspapers, that describe your most positive qualities. (*Example: artistic, smart, caring, love for children, etc.*) **Place them in the appropriate boxes below.**

My Personality Strengths

My Talents

My Knowledge

My Special Gifts

My Strengths and Talents

Many teens who have been through a traumatic event lose track of their strengths, talents, and positive personality traits. Many of these losses are due to the experience they endured, but some are not.

In the spaces that follow, identify your strengths and talents.

My Strengths	**My Talents**	**My Positive Personality Traits**
EX.: Caring about others	*Drawing and painting*	*I am conscientious at school*

_____   _____   _____

_____   _____   _____

_____   _____   _____

_____   _____   _____

_____   _____   _____

How did the traumatic event make you stronger?

_____

_____

_____

_____

How did the traumatic event help you discover that you have more talents?

_____

_____

_____

_____

How did the traumatic event strengthen you to be more able to deal with life in general?

_____

_____

_____

_____

Managing Trauma Workbook for Teens

Re-Writing Your Narrative

In the space that follows, you have an opportunity to re-write the narrative of the traumatic event you experienced.

For this activity, describe the event, but this time describe yourself as the hero/heroine of the story. Use Name Codes.

Would this have been possible? _____

What did you learn? _____

_____

My Transition

Solving My Problem

To recover, one needs to be able to solve problems well. Worrying about your problems will not only fail to solve them, but it will also create additional stress. It is important to develop a system for solving the small or large problems you encounter in life.

Identify a problem you have encountered in life. Use Name Codes. _____

_____

_____

What are the elements of the problem? Who is involved? What happened?

_____

_____

_____

What are some possible solutions to your problem? Don't evaluate, just write them down.

_____   _____

_____   _____

_____   _____

What are the pros and cons of each of these solutions?

- What is required to implement the solution?
- Do I have the time, money and skills to carry the solution out?
- Can the solution be implemented?
- Would the people involved be cooperative?

After you have answered the previous questions for each solution, put a "Yes" or "No" next to each solution above.

Which solution provides you with the best chance of success? Why this solution?

_____

_____

_____

Managing Trauma Workbook for Teens

My Wish

Having a specific wish in life can help you move on from your traumatic event.

**In each of the spaces that follow, describe various aspects of your wish.
If the sentence starter does not apply to you, explain why not. Use Name Codes.**

My wish is ...
_____
_____

My education contributes to my wish in the following ways:
_____
_____

My family contributes to my wish in the following ways:
_____
_____

My interests contribute to my wish in the following ways:
_____
_____

My job or volunteer work contributes to my wish in the following ways:
_____
_____

My friends contribute to my wish in the following ways:
_____
_____

My heart's desire contributes to my wish in the following ways:
_____
_____

My _____ contributes to my wish in the following ways:
_____
_____

My Transition

Add Life Structure

To avoid as many triggers as possible, it is important to add structure to your life as much as possible, and to eliminate chance and chaos as much as possible.

In each of the areas, how can you structure your life to have fewer triggers?

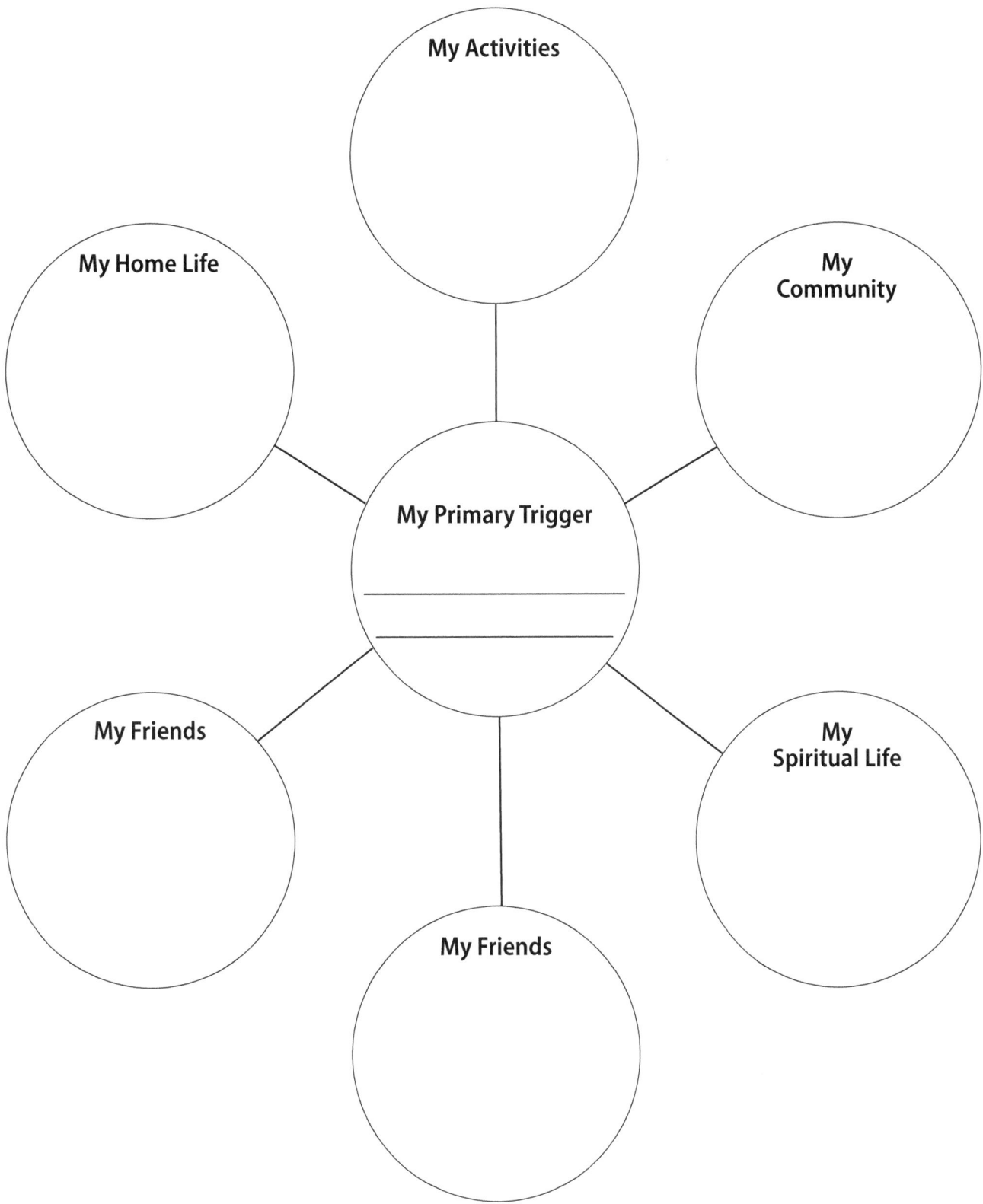

MODULE IV

My Coping Tools

The memory, experiencing and re-experiencing, has such power over one's mere personal life …

~ Rebecca West

Name _____

Date_____

Participants can place the activities in this module in a "Coping Journal" notebook for their further reference.

Managing Trauma Workbook for Teens

Skills Emphasized in Each Activity Handout

Intrusive Thoughts .... page 88
   Identify, quantify, and reframe eight intrusive thoughts.

My Trauma Triggers .... page 89
   Describe these triggers: sensory, physical, emotional, and special events.

Trigger Management .... page 90
   Select six coping skills one has tried, and why they were liked/disliked.

My Nightmare and My Trauma .... page 91
   Share the dream's triggers, after-effects, and ways it interferes with activities.

The Value of Positive Distractions .... page 92
   State five unwanted thoughts, distractions, which works best, and why.

Flashbacks .... page 93
   Describe one's flashback – its timing, triggers, the persons involved and ways to cope.

My Sleep Patterns .... page 94
   Quantify the extent of one's sleep problem. Research restful sleep tips.

Tracking My Sleep Patterns .... page 95
   Note effects of routines and events on sleep quantity/quality for a week.

Sleep Tips .... page 96
   From thirty-nine tips, select those that help, and tips one is willing to try.

Jittery, Anxious? Edgy? Jumpy? Agitated? Worried? Scared? Skittish? ..... page 97
   State what elicits the responses, prior reactions, and ways to gain perspective.

Over-Cautious? .... page 98
   Select eight examples of own over-caution, reasons, and ways to cope.

Problem Solving for Overly-Cautious Behavior .... page 99
   Share how to handle five or more problematic reactions.

Anticipating High-Risk Situations .... page 100
   Describe five high-risk situations, reactions, and steps to reduce stress.

COPING: Let's Meditate .... page 101
   Perform three steps in response to a stressful thought; evaluate effects.

COPING: Deep Breathing .... page 102
   Perform two steps, list five benefits, tell how to use the skill when memories intrude.

COPING: Mindfulness and Paying Attention .... page 103
   Perform four steps. Journal about feelings, effects, and ways the process helps.

COPING: Total-Body Relaxation .... page 104
   Perform seventeen Progressive Muscle Relaxation steps.

Ways to Make Meaning .... page 105
   Identify nine ways one was helped by the trauma.

My Coping Tools Scale
Introduction and Directions

Healing from a trauma is often accomplished when the trauma is processed and accepted as a part of your life experiences, part of what makes you who you are today. Many teens want to escape from their painful memories, only to find that memories are triggered by many ordinary life occurrences and will continue to reoccur. By being aware of this, one can learn to manage symptoms.

This scale contains 30 statements related to how you re-experience the memories of the trauma in your life. Read each of the statements and decide how much the statement describes you.

- If the statement describes you a lot, circle the number under that column next to that item.
- If the statement describes you sometimes, circle the number under that column next to that item.
- If the statement describes you only a little or not at all, circle the number under that column next to that item.

In the following example, the circled number under "A Lot" indicates the statement is highly descriptive of the person completing the scale a lot of the time.

WHEN I BEGIN TO RE-EXPERIENCE MY TRAUMA …	A LOT	SOMETIMES	LITTLE/NONE
I am not able to remember details of the event	(3)	2	1

This is not a test. Since there are no right or wrong answers, do not spend too much time thinking about your answers. Be sure to respond to every statement.

(Turn to the next page and begin.)

My Coping Tools Scale

WHEN I BEGIN TO RE-EXPERIENCE MY TRAUMA …	A LOT	SOMETIMES	LITTLE/NONE
I am not able to remember details of the event	3	2	1
I am jumpy and jittery	3	2	1
I am overprotective of those I love	3	2	1
I am so fearful I can't concentrate	3	2	1
I am unusually cautious	3	2	1
I become lightheaded or dizzy	3	2	1
I can hardly breathe or I breathe rapidly	3	2	1
I cannot cope with the memories	3	2	1
I can't feel calm, even in safe places	3	2	1
I experience unwanted memories of my trauma	3	2	1
I fear my scary nightmares and don't know what they mean	3	2	1
I feel like the trauma is happening to me right now	3	2	1
I feel my blood pressure rising	3	2	1
I feel my chest tightening	3	2	1
I feel my heart beating faster	3	2	1
I feel on guard at all times	3	2	1
I feel tingling in my hands or have sweaty palms	3	2	1
I find that unexpected things trigger my memories of the event	3	2	1
I have flashbacks of the event	3	2	1
I have hallucination-like nightmares about the event	3	2	1
I have stomach issues	3	2	1
I try to go to sleep but keep remembering	3	2	1
I look for exits in stores, movies and restaurants	3	2	1
I scan over my shoulder a lot	3	2	1
I scare easily	3	2	1
I sense reliving the moment of the event	3	2	1
I start crying when I remember	3	2	1
I suffer from pains in different parts of my body	3	2	1
I sweat profusely	3	2	1
I want to have a weapon with me at all times	3	2	1

TOTAL = _____

(Go to the Scoring Directions.)

My Coping Tools Scale
Scoring Directions

Your ability to move past the trauma that you have experienced largely depends on your ability to recall your memories in enough detail to explore what really happened and integrate the experience into your other memories. This scale is designed to help you understand and identify the symptoms when you begin to re-experience symptoms of your trauma.

Add the numbers that you circled. Your total will range from 30 to 90.
Then, transfer this total to the space below:

Re-Experiencing Symptoms Total _____

Profile Interpretation

Individual Score	Result	Indications
30 - 49	Low	Low scores indicate that you are experiencing a low level of symptoms. Complete the following exercises to ensure that you reduce your symptoms even further.
50 - 70	Moderate	Moderate scores indicate that you are experiencing a medium to high level of symptoms. Complete the following exercises to ensure that you reduce your symptoms even further.
71 - 90	High	High scores indicate that you are experiencing a very high level of symptoms. Complete the following exercises to that ensure you reduce your symptoms even further.

Scale Description

Teens scoring high on this scale may be re-experiencing their trauma through symptoms related to their body; re-experiencing them through memories and flashbacks; and re-experiencing them through their intuition. Some people experience the opposite – emotional numbness, and they mentally block out the event.

They are constantly reminded of their traumatic event.

Intrusive Thoughts

Following are some of the most intrusive thoughts that people who have experienced trauma tend to have. Which ones do you experience?

Complete the table that follows. If these thoughts do not occur to you, just write N/A (Does Not Apply). Use Name Codes.

My Thoughts	How Often I Have These Thoughts	How I Can Reframe These Thoughts
EXAMPLE: I am a victim.	Every time the least little negative thing happens to me, I feel out of control of my life.	Everyone experiences stress. I can handle it and take control of my life.
I am a victim.		
My troubles are the fault of others.		
My troubles are in part my own fault.		
I can't trust people anymore.		
Other people blame me.		
I'll never feel safe again.		
It will happen again.		
I'm a coward.		
Other		
Other		

Which of the thoughts interfere with your life enough to interfere with your daily activities?

How can you overcome these types of thoughts?

My Coping Tools

My Trauma Triggers

It is important to explore the triggers of stressful reactions after you have experienced a trauma.

The following will help you examine what reminds you of your trauma.

Place an X in the boxes that apply to you.
Then, on the line after each item you marked, describe how the item applies to you.
The area with the most boxes checked is your greatest source of triggers.

- ☐ When I see _____
- ☐ When I hear _____
- ☐ When I smell _____
- ☐ When I taste _____
- ☐ When I feel _____

Senses TOTAL = _____

- ☐ When I move a certain way _____
- ☐ When my body is in a certain position_____
- ☐ When I am touched a certain way _____
- ☐ When I feel internal sensations (headache, heartbeat)_____
- ☐ When I feel tension _____

Physical TOTAL = _____

- ☐ When I see or hear about a sad situation _____
- ☐ When certain seasons come along _____
- ☐ When I feel threatened in any way _____
- ☐ When important dates are upcoming _____
- ☐ When a certain time of day approaches _____

Emotional TOTAL = _____

- ☐ When I feel really stressed _____
- ☐ When I am in a situation similar to the situation in which the trauma occurred _____
- ☐ When I argue with others _____
- ☐ When I experience a major change in my life _____
- ☐ When I experience a disruption to everyday activities _____

Stressful Events TOTAL = _____

Managing Trauma Workbook for Teens

Trigger Management

Rather than giving in to the distress caused by intrusive thoughts, it is better to try and manage the stress.

Think back over the past week. Describe which types of coping mechanisms you used, how effective they were, and the end result. Complete this table to identify effective trigger-management techniques. **Use Name Codes.**

Techniques	Tried and Liked it. Why I Like it.	Have Not Tried it. Why I Haven't.	Tried it and Do Not Like it. Why I Don't.
EXAMPLE: Relaxation	*When I feel a trigger to my trauma, I take out my cell phone, put on my head phones, and listen to relaxing music.*		
Relaxation – Find a quiet place to relax, meditate, yoga, soothing music, guided imagery, draw, write, etc.			
Breathing – Take some time to simply breathe. Take deep breaths in through your nose and breathe out through your mouth.			
Prescribed Medications -- Be sure that you have taken your medications that were prescribed by a physician.			
Visualization – Think about your safe place and visualize that you are there and feel totally relaxed and safe.			
Social Support – Confide in and talk with trusted friends and family about your stress and anxiety.			
Distract Myself in a Healthy Manner – Find healthy ways to take your mind off your anxiety.			
Other			
Other			
Other			

My Coping Tools

Nightmare and My Trauma

Many teens who have experienced trauma have recurring nightmares that interfere with sleep.

Explore the effects of your nightmare. Use Name Codes.

What is your nightmare? _____

_____

_____

_____

Do you know what triggers your nightmare? _____

What is it? _____

_____

_____

_____

_____

_____

How does your nightmare affect you afterwards? _____

_____

_____

_____

_____

_____

How does your nightmare interfere with your next day's activities? _____

_____

_____

_____

_____

It helps to understand nightmares. Who is a trusting person with whom you can talk about your nightmares? _____

Why this person? _____

_____

_____

_____

The Value of Positive Distractions

Distracting yourself from unwanted thoughts may help take your mind off your trauma.

What are some positive ways you can distract yourself? Use Name Codes.

My Unwanted Thoughts	How I Can Distract Myself	How This Can Helps Me
Example: It happening again!	I can text one of my friends on my cell phone.	I get absorbed in our conversation and not my trauma.

Which positive distractions work best for you and why?

_____

_____

Flashbacks

Flashbacks occur when you feel as if a trauma from the past takes you back, and is occurring to you in the here and now.

Think back to the last time you experienced a flashback and answer questions below. Use Name Codes.

When a flashback occurs, what time of day does it usually happen?
_____
_____
_____

Where does it usually happen?
_____
_____
_____
_____
_____

Who is usually involved when it occurs?
_____
_____
_____

What do you think triggers it?
_____
_____
_____

What can you do the next time it happens?
_____
_____
_____
_____
_____

My Sleep Patterns

You might have trouble falling asleep and staying asleep. By exploring your sleep patterns, you can discover some of the reasons you are not getting adequate amounts of sleep.

For the assessment below, rate your sleep patterns by circling the appropriate number.

1 = If it happens very seldom or not at all
2 = If it happens some of the time
3 = If it happens most of the time

I have trouble falling asleep at night	3	2	1
I awaken too early in the morning	3	2	1
I don't do well at school or at work because I'm tired	3	2	1
I have scary nightmares or night terrors	3	2	1
I am restless while sleeping	3	2	1
I wake up in a few hours and then can't go back to sleep	3	2	1
I dream weird dreams	3	2	1
I am sleepy during the day	3	2	1
I feel tired when I wake up	3	2	1
I have body movements with my bad dreams	3	2	1
I have nightmares early and then I am too upset to sleep	3	2	1
I can't fall asleep because I have unwanted thoughts	3	2	1
I rarely get a good night's sleep	3	2	1
I awaken and then think unhappy thoughts	3	2	1
I sleep walk	3	2	1

Now add the total of the numbers you circled above.
If your total score was between 15 and 25, you probably are having some sleep problems.
If your total score was between 26 and 35, you are probably having many sleep problems.
If your total score was between 36 and 45, you are probably having major sleep problems.

Using the Internet, research some things you can do to sleep more thoroughly at night.

My Coping Tools

Tracking My Sleep Patterns

If you are experiencing sleep problems, it may be helpful for you to keep track of exactly how much sleep you get each night. A sleep journal can help you to identify the days when you do not get adequate or restful sleep, and the possible reasons.

Complete the following sleep diary information each night for at least two weeks.

Day of the Week	Total Hours of Sleep	My Bedtime Routine	Quality of Sleep 1 = not good 5 = great	What happened this day related to my trauma
Monday				
Tuesday				
Wednesday				
Thursday				
Friday				
Saturday				
Sunday				

What is the relationship between your bedtime routine and what happens during the day and while you sleep?_____

_____

_____

Managing Trauma Workbook for Teens

Sleep Tips

If you are not getting restorative or adequate sleep at night, you need to work to improve your chances of good sleep. The good news is that you can do a many things to improve your chances of getting better sleep.

Some of the techniques you can try to improve your sleep at night are listed below.

Put a check (•) by each one that has been effective for you.

Put a plus (+) after each one that you are willing to try.

- ☐ Avoid drinking too many liquids at night
- ☐ Be sure your bed is comfortable
- ☐ Before bedtime, prepare for the next day: clothes picked out, homework completed, lunch packed, etc.
- ☐ Block out noises with earplugs
- ☐ Decide to have no rich foods within two hours of bedtime
- ☐ Do gentle stretches before bed
- ☐ Do not eat spicy foods in the evening
- ☐ Don't watch television one to two hours before sleep
- ☐ Eat a light snack if you are hungry at bedtime
- ☐ Eliminate loud noises
- ☐ Engage in something mildly stimulating after dinner to avoid falling asleep too early
- ☐ Enjoy a warm bath or shower before bed
- ☐ Exercise regularly 20-30 minutes in the morning or early afternoon, not at night
- ☐ Go to sleep at the same time each day
- ☐ Have the same sleep routine on weekends
- ☐ If taking a nap, do it in the early afternoon
- ☐ Journal
- ☐ Keep TVs or computers from the bedroom
- ☐ Listen to a book on tape
- ☐ Maintain a bedtime routine
- ☐ Make sure the room temperature is set for comfort
- ☐ Meditate
- ☐ Mentally, repeat soothing words
- ☐ No tablets or smart phones in the bedroom
- ☐ Provide only a soft light in the bedroom
- ☐ Read a book or magazine
- ☐ Relax with progressive relaxation exercise
- ☐ Resist caffeine after noon time
- ☐ Rest to relaxing music
- ☐ Say no to alcohol and nicotine before bedtime
- ☐ Set the temperature or open windows for a cool room
- ☐ Stay away from big meals close to bedtime
- ☐ Take medications as prescribed
- ☐ Try deep breathing exercise
- ☐ Use guided imagery
- ☐ Wake up at the same time each day
- ☐ When you wake up and can't go back to sleep in 15 minutes, do a non-stimulating activity
- ☐ Wind down the evening with a favorite hobby
- ☐ Write ideas and plans on paper next to the bed before going to sleep
- ☐ Other suggestions?_____

_____

My Coping Tools

Jittery? Anxious? Edgy? Jumpy? Agitated? Worried? Scared? Skittish?

Often when people are overly cautious because of their trauma, they become more jittery, anxious, edgy, jumpy, agitated, worried, scared and/or skittish than usual.

My trauma? _____
(Example: I almost drowned when a boy pushed me in the pool in the 7 foot water.)

Below, write the types of noises, actions, or events that affect you more than usual. What happens and what can you do about it? **Use Name Codes**.

The noise, action, or event that affects me,	When this happens, I feel …	To put this situation in perspective I can …
Example: When I'm in the lake and a big wave comes.	*Scared - I feel like I can't breathe.*	*Remember that I can now swim.*

Managing Trauma Workbook for Teens

Over-Cautious?

Often teens who have experienced a traumatic event become over-cautious.
However, this can be taken to an extreme and cause more anxiety and fear than necessary.

Explore ways you may be over-cautious. Use Name Codes.

Ways I am Over-Cautious	Why I Feel Like This	How I can Avoid being Over-Cautious
EXAMPLE: I feel like I'm on guard all of the time.	*I am scared that the trauma situation will happen again!*	*Replace my over-the-top negative thoughts with reality-based thoughts.*
I feel like I'm on guard all of the time.		
I am too cautious.		
I always look over my shoulder.		
I am overprotective.		
I don't feel safe.		
I startle easily.		
I don't trust others.		
I am ready to flee.		
Other		

Which of your over-cautious behaviors concerns you the most? What will you do about it?

_____

_____

_____

My Coping Tools

Problem Solving for the Overly-Cautious

Constantly scanning the environment for signs of danger can be a problematic for survivors of traumatic experiences.

In the spaces that follow, write about how acting overly-cautious makes your life stressful. Use Name Codes.

Overly-Cautious	Why This Presents a Problem To Me in My Life	What I Can Do About It
EXAMPLE: After nearly drowning, I am very scared when I am near large bodies of water.	I can't go swimming with my friends because I am afraid.	I can learn to use coping methods such as meditation or deep breathing.
I am in a perpetual state of fear when_____		
I don't feel prepared to cope with _____		
I am worried I will be too preoccupied about _____		
I am unable to connect with others because _____		
I am missing out on _____ _____ when others in my life _____		
Other _____		

© 2015 WHOLE PERSON ASSOCIATES, 101 W. 2ND ST., SUITE 203, DULUTH MN 55802 • 800-247-6789

Managing Trauma Workbook for Teens

Anticipating High-Risk Situations

There are avoidable triggers of your trauma. It is important to be aware of and to identify your high-risk situations, and be prepared to deal with the stress that will arise.

What are your high-risk situations and how can you cope with them more effectively? Use Name Codes.

My High-Risk Situations	When I Encounter this Situation	How I React	How I Can Cope
EXAMPLE: Walking at night.	I love to go to high school football games, but get nervous walking to my car after the games by myself.	I get sweaty, begin to feel dizzy, and have trouble breathing.	Find a way to park closer to the stadium, and ask friends to walk with me.

What high-risk situation is particularly worrisome? _____
_____
_____

What steps can you take immediately to feel less stressed if you're in that situation? _____
_____
_____

What do you do to be sure you're not in this situation in the future? _____
_____
_____

My Coping Tools

COPING: Let's Meditate

There are many misconceptions about what meditation is and how to meditate. Meditation is easy and helps you relax, become calm and stop the thoughts about the event from flooding back into your consciousness.

Here is the process:
1. Right now, think of something that is calming to you, such as sitting on a beach, a vase full of flowers, your favorite pet, walking in the woods, or the face of someone you love.
2. With this image in your mind, gently close your eyes and focus on this image.
3. After a few seconds, open your eyes.

How did it feel?

_____
_____
_____
_____

What thoughts popped back into your head?

_____
_____
_____
_____

4. Now try again and this time as the thoughts pop into your head, let them dissolve and re-focus your attention on the image.

How did it feel now?

_____
_____
_____
_____

Keep practicing this daily for five to ten minutes, and you will notice your anxiety becoming less prominent.

Managing Trauma Workbook for Teens

COPING: Deep Breathing

> *When you own your breath, nobody can steal your peace.*
> ~ **Author Unknown**

Deep breathing can help you in a variety of ways:
- Reduces hyperventilation when you encounter a trigger
- Helps you feel more at peace
- Helps you sleep better
- Reduces everyday stress
- Reduces panic and anxiety

Try all 3 of these relaxation techniques.
A. Scan your body and identify the parts that are the most tense. Next, inhale slowly through your nose until you see your abdomen rising. Hold this breath for five seconds. Then, exhale through your mouth slowly, pushing all of the air out. Do this again five times until you feel more relaxed.
B. Breathe in slowly for five seconds. Exhale slowly for 7 seconds. Repeat three times. Roll shoulders back and be confident to face the world.
C. Picture a large canister that needs to be filled up with air. The first breath we will fill about 1/4 of the canister, the 2nd breath we will fill up to almost 2/3 of the canister, and then with the final breath we will fill the canister completely – using breathing in through the nose and pushing breath out through the mouth. Make a sound as you're pushing the air out.

Which technique worked best for you? A, B, or C? _____

How can you use this technique when a trigger causes you to remember the trauma?
_____
_____
_____

What obstacles do you anticipate in using this technique and how can you overcome them?
_____
_____
_____

What benefits do you anticipate in using this technique?
_____
_____
_____

My Coping Tools

COPING: Mindfulness and Paying Attention

Mindfulness is the skill of attending fully to any experience you encounter. Being mindful can lessen the impact and help you to step back from thoughts and feelings about your trauma without reacting.

Let's practice mindfulness now.
1. Look around you and focus on something of interest to you.
2. Concentrate on the object.
3. Each time your mind begins to wander from the object, bring it back to full attention.
4. Do this for several minutes.
5. Then journal about the following questions.

How did you feel during the activity?

_____

_____

_____

Did you have difficulty attending to the object? If so, why?

_____

_____

_____

What did you notice about your thoughts as you mindfully attended to the object?

_____

_____

_____

How can this help you?

_____

_____

_____

COPING: Total-Body Relaxation

Anxiety manifests itself through physical symptoms in your body. These physical symptoms often reinforce your anxiety-producing thoughts and feelings. Total-Body Relaxation (often called Progressive Muscle Relaxation) is a simple technique used to stop anxiety by relaxing all of the muscles throughout your body one group at a time.

Read through the following script several times before you attempt to do this exercise.

1. *Take a few deep breaths, and begin to relax.*
2. *Get comfortable and put aside all of your worries.*
3. *Let each part of your body begin to relax ... starting with your feet.*
4. *Imagine your feet relaxing as all of your tension begins to fade away.*
5. *Imagine the relaxation moving up into your calves and thighs ... feel them beginning to relax.*
6. *Continue now to let the relaxation move into your hips.*
7. *Allow the relaxation to move into your waist.*
8. *Your entire body from the waist down is now completely relaxed.*
9. *Let go of any strain and discomfort you might feel.*
10. *Allow the relaxation to move into your chest until your chest feels completely relaxed.*
11. *Just enjoy the feeling of complete relaxation.*
12. *Continue to let the relaxation move through the muscles of your shoulders, then spread down into your upper arms, into your elbows, and finally all the way down to your wrists and hands.*
13. *Put aside all of your worries.*
14. *Let yourself be totally present in the moment and let yourself relax more and more. Let all the muscles in your neck unwind and let the relaxation move into your chin and jaws.*
15. *Feel the tension around your eyes flow away as the relaxation moves throughout your face and head.*
16. *Feel your forehead relax and your entire head beginning to feel lighter.*
17. *Let yourself drift deeper and deeper into relaxation and peace.*

After you have read the above script several times, find a quiet location where you can practice Total-Body Relaxation.

Assume a comfortable position in a chair, on a table, or on the floor.

Take off your jewelry and glasses so that you are totally free.

Try to let the relaxation happen without having to force it.

If during the relaxation you lose concentration, don't be concerned - just begin again.

My Coping Tools

Ways to Make Meaning

As a result of the trauma you have experienced, you are changed. An important aspect in healing is to make sense of the trauma that happened to you.

**Think about ways that you have grown from the trauma, and answer the following sentence starters that apply to you. If any do not apply to you, explain in that space.
Use Name Codes.**

I can tolerate anything else that happens to me including _____
_____
_____

I can see a cause that I could volunteer for such as _____
_____
_____

I will take care of myself for the rest of my life by _____
_____
_____

I have changed for the better in the following ways: _____
_____
_____

I accept that what happened to me was not my fault and _____
_____
_____

I have greater will power than I thought, and it shows up when I _____
_____
_____

I am more persistent as evidenced by _____
_____
_____

I am closer to the following people: _____
_____
_____

I feel like my purpose in life is to _____
_____
_____

MODULE V

Erasing the Stigma of Mental Health Issues

Stigma's power lies in silence. The silence that persists when discussion and action should be taking place ...

~ M. B. Dallocchio

Name _____

Date _____

Managing Trauma Workbook for Teens

Skills Emphasized in Each Activity Handout

Two Types of Mental Health Stigma .... page 110
Describe types of stigma and prejudice endured due to trauma.

The Stigma of Trauma – THE PAST .... page 111
Share feelings about past disclosures.

The Stigma of Trauma – THE PRESENT .... page 112
Identify gains and losses, whom to tell, and how.

Speak Your Mind .... page 113
Personalize a quotation about independent thinking by responding to five questions.

If We Stamp Out the Stigma ... . page 114
Journal about a quote to help shed shame and fear.

Glenn Close said ... . page 115
State ways talking about issues promotes healing.

Effects of Trauma Issues .... page 116
Name eight persons who may help in stigma-related situations.

The Stigma of Going to a Mental Health Therapist .... page 117
Discuss concerns; commit to seeing a counselor if needed.

Stereotypes .... page 118
Document ways one refutes six stereotypes.

Will You Speak Out? .... page 119
Describe ways individuals and the group can help erase stigma.

My Negative Thoughts .... page 120
Identify six negative assumptions; use a physical thought-stopping technique.

Focus on Your Strengths .... page 121
State ways to demonstrate strengths in five areas of life.

Ways I Try to Minimize My Trauma Stress .... page 122
Respond to six examples: tell effects on self, others, and better ways to cope.

Ways I am Treated .... page 123
Describe eight ways one is treated, plus self-treatment.

Self-Doubt .... page 124
Describe five ways to stop the self-defeating process.

A Poster about the STIGMA of People Who Have Experienced a Trauma .... page 125
Show perceptions of being stigmatized due to trauma.

A Poster about ACCEPTANCE of People Who Have Experienced a Trauma .... page 126
Show how reaction to trauma looks when one is accepted.

DE-STIGMA-TIZE with the Facts about Mental Health Issues .... page 127
Acknowledge eight myths, corresponding facts, and the value of seeking help.

Coping with the Stigma of a Mental Health Issue .... page 128
Personalize five suggestions; state ways to follow through.

Speak Out Against Stigmas .... page 129
State five ways to advocate and the benefits to self and others.

Erasing the Stigma of Mental Health Issues
Introduction

A stigma is "extreme social disapproval of some type of personal characteristic or a belief that is not considered socially acceptable." People who have a particular attribute considered unwanted by society are rejected or stigmatized as a result of the attribute. Teens who have experienced traumatic events in the past are often judged unfairly to be personally responsible, crazy, violent, unpredictable, explosive, aggressive and/or unstable. These judgments, or social stigmas, can cause people who experience these issues to feel devalued as human beings. They are often ostracized from activities, rejected in social situations, stereotyped, minimized in the workplace, and shunned by others. Teens experiencing the stigma of reactions to traumatic events often feel extreme physical, emotional and psychological distress.

Teens who stigmatize and/or stereotype others bring about unfair treatment rather than help. This unfair treatment can be very obvious. For example, people make negative comments or laugh. On the other hand, this unfair treatment can be very subtle. For example - people assume that a person who experiences a traumatic event is dangerous, violent, depressed, or out-of-control - and they avoid or shun that person.

Stigmas affect a large percentage of people throughout the world. Some of the more common stigmas are associated with physical disabilities, mental health issues, age, body type, gender, sexual orientation, nationality, religion, spirituality, family, ethnicity, race, financial status, social sub-cultures, and conduct. Stigmas set people apart from society and produce feelings in them of shame and isolation. Teens who are stigmatized are often considered socially unacceptable, and suffer prejudice, rejection, avoidance and discrimination.

WHAT CAN BE DONE?
Fear of judgment and ridicule about unwanted thoughts, feelings and actions often compel individuals and their families to hide from society rather than face criticism, shunning, labeling and stereotyping. Instead of seeking treatment, they struggle in silence. Let's discuss some ways you can combat the stereotypes and stigmas associated with these issues.

- You and your loved ones have choices. You can decide who is to know about your trauma and what to tell them. You need not feel guilty, ashamed or embarrassed.
- You are not alone. Remember that many other people are coping with a similar situation.
- Look into or start a support group to meet others who experience what you do.
- Seek help and remember that the activities in this workbook and treatment from medical professionals can help you to have a productive education and career, and live a satisfying life.
- Be proactive and surround yourself with supportive people – people you can trust. Social isolation is a negative side effect of the stigma linked to reactions to traumatic events. Isolating yourself and discontinuing enjoyable activities will not help.

HOW CAN THIS SECTION HELP ME?
Managing Trauma Workbook for Teens is designed to help you deal more effectively with your issues, and this section is specifically designed to help you overcome the stigma attached to those issues. Complete the activities that follow to help you to appreciate yourself, feel content, and become more resilient in the face of your trauma issues.

Two Types of Mental Health Stigma

Mental health stigma can be divided into two types:

1. **Social stigma** is characterized by prejudicial attitudes and discriminating behavior directed towards individuals with mental health issues.
   (Example: Being excluded from a team because it happened.)

2. **Perceived stigma** is the internalizing by the people with mental health issues of their understanding of discrimination.
   (Example: I am damaged because of the trauma.)

What do you think are the main differences between these two types of stigmas?

_____
_____
_____
_____

Describe a time when you faced prejudice or discrimination because you experienced a traumatic event.

_____
_____
_____
_____

Describe a time when you felt like you were at a disadvantage because you experienced a traumatic event.

_____
_____
_____
_____

Often one perceives others' stigmatizing, or exaggerates others' or their own reactions.

Erasing the Stigma of Mental Health Issues

The Stigma of Trauma
THE PAST

Teens who experience a traumatic event in their lives are prone to reoccurring symptoms. When this happens, they often have a stigma placed on them by other people or by themselves. Often the stigma attached to these issues stops one from moving forward - being unable to talk about it for fear of being judged or labeled. We can erase the stigma of any mental health issues by starting to discuss it with one person at a time, and taking the time to explain the traumatic events you lived through in the past.

Let's start with people with whom you have already shared your story. Use Name Codes.

With whom have you discussed your issues? USE NAME CODES	What did you say?	What was this person's reaction? What did the person say?	How did you feel?
Family			
Friends			
Acquaintances			
People in your community or your house of worship			
Mental health Professionals			
Other			

If any one of the above reacted in a negative way, to what do you attribute that reaction?

_____

_____

_____

The Stigma of Trauma
THE PRESENT

If you are willing to tell your story to people, now may be the time. This workbook has helped you to organize your thoughts and feelings about what happened to you. One of the ways to erase this stigma is to talk about it and let others know that people who have these issues are just like anyone else who have some type of an issue.

Perhaps it is time to talk with other people whom you trust and/or with whom you feel safe. Use Name Codes.

Person with whom you might discuss your issue?	What would you say to this person?	What do you think this person's reaction might be?	What could you gain or lose by discussing it with this person?
Family			
Friends			
Acquaintances			
People in your community or your house of worship			
Mental health Professionals			
Other			

Role-play the above relationships.
Brainstorm this with the group:
At what point, in a serious relationship, is it time to discuss your issues?

Erasing the Stigma of Mental Health Issues

Speak Your Mind

> *Follow the path of the unsafe, independent thinker. Expose your ideas to the danger of controversy. Speak your mind and fear less the label of 'crackpot' than the stigma of conformity.*
>
> **~ Thomas J. Watson**

What does this quote mean to you? _____
_____
_____

Have you spoken your mind? Why not? _____
_____
_____

Are you worried about being labeled? _____
_____
_____

How can you expose your ideas to others? _____
_____
_____

What is keeping you from telling your story? _____
_____
_____

If We Stamp Out the Stigma …

Journal your thoughts about the following quotation and describe how you can do your part to erase the stigma of trauma issues.

> *If we stamp out the stigma attached to mental health issues, shed the shame and eliminate the fear, then we open the door for people to speak freely about what they are feeling and thinking.*
>
> **~ Jaletta Albright Desmond**

Erasing the Stigma of Mental Health Issues

Glenn Close said ...

The most powerful way to change someone's view is to meet them ... People who do come out and talk about mental illness, that's when healing can really begin. You can lead a productive life.

Name a time when you have changed someone else's view – about anything. _____
_____
_____

How did that feel to you? _____
_____
_____

Name a time you were tempted to talk about your trauma issues, but didn't? Why not? _____
_____
_____

Write about a situation in which you DID talk about your trauma issues. _____
_____
_____
_____
_____

How did that feel? _____
How did it work out? _____
_____

Anyone else? _____
Who is a trusted person you can ask for a referral of someone to talk with in order to begin to heal?
_____

Anyone else? _____
In an ideal world, how can you lead a more stable life? _____
_____
_____

How can you contribute to changing stigma? _____
_____
_____

Managing Trauma Workbook for Teens

Effects of Trauma Issues

Check out these harmful effects of the stigma of traumatic events. On the lines next to each item, explain if it has affected you in some way and how. Use Name Codes.

1. Lack of understanding by family. _____
   _____

2. Lack of understanding by friends. _____
   _____

3. Lack of understanding by co-workers, supervisors and/or customers. _____
   _____

4. Discrimination at work. _____
   _____

5. Inability to join community programs. _____
   _____

6. Abuse: physical, emotional, verbal or sexual. _____
   _____

7. Pressure from friends. _____
   _____

8. The belief that you will never be able to succeed or that you can't improve your situation. _____
   _____

**On the line of the corresponding number, write the NAME CODE of a person you can speak to, a person who might help to support you about each of the situations you noted above.
Add a reason for each person you have chosen.**

1. _____
2. _____
3. _____
4. _____
5. _____
6. _____
7. _____
8. _____

Erasing the Stigma of Mental Health Issues

The Stigma of Going to a Mental Health Therapist

Many people have pre-conceived ideas about anyone seeking therapy.

If you know of anyone who has gone to a mental health therapist, write what you know about the experience. _____
_____
_____

Here are some facts about mental health and mental health therapy.

- Mental health includes how you act, feel, and think in different situations.
- Mental health problems can be caused by many different things including medical health issues, abuse (emotional, physical, verbal, sexual), stress, worry, loss of a relationship, food issues, self-injuries, ADHD, STD's, family changes, addictions, traumatic events, problems, self-confidence, etc.
- If someone goes to a mental health therapist, this does NOT mean the person is crazy. Doctors and mental health therapists treat people the same as any other doctor treats problems (broken leg, diabetes, cancer).
- There needs to be a good connection between you and the therapist. Your therapist should be someone you feel you can trust.
- This might take a few meetings and/or a few therapists, to find the right one for you.
- Non-judgmental people who truly care about you will not judge you in a negative way. They will be proud of you for seeking help.
- A therapist does not assume that you have a mental illness. The therapist assumes something is troubling you, knows that no one leads a perfect life, and admires you for trying to make changes in your life.
- The therapist's job is to help you understand what's going on.
- The therapist will not tell you how to live your life, or how to think, act or believe.
- The therapist is not an advice-giver, but will help you think about how to improve your quality of life.
- The therapist may have some thoughts, and with you, will help you make changes.
- The therapist can help you to increase your life management skills.
- The therapist will help you recognize and express your feelings in a healthy way.
- The only person who can "fix" your problems is you, but a therapist will help you with an action plan.
- The mental health therapist may suggest that you see a medical doctor for medication.
- Therapy can be a slow or long process. Being open and honest and wanting to feel better will make the difference.

Place an X by the facts that you did not know before.

What stops you from talking with a mental health therapist?_____
_____
_____
_____

After learning about these facts, can you make a commitment to speak with a counselor or therapist?

*signature*_____

Managing Trauma Workbook for Teens

Stereotypes

The social stigmas about trauma often translate into the following inaccurate stereotypes.

Below, write about how you are unlike the stereotype provided. Use Name Codes.

Stereotype	How I Defy that Stereotype
They are damaged	
They show no emotions	
They have a victim mentality	
They can't do things	
They feel entitled	
They want people to feel sorry for them	
Other stereotypes of trauma stress	

What would you like to say to other people who label you with these or other stereotypical words?

_____

_____

_____

Will You Speak Out?

> *Ten people who speak make more noise than ten thousand who are silent.*
> ~ Napoleon Bonaparte

How can YOU speak out to erase the stigma of mental health issues?

_____
_____
_____
_____
_____
_____
_____
_____
_____
_____

Brainstorm with a few other people about how your group can speak out to erase the stigma of mental health issues.

_____
_____
_____
_____
_____
_____
_____
_____
_____
_____

My Negative Thoughts

You can begin to overcome the stigma related to trauma issues by refusing to worry about what others think. When you are worried about what others say about you, or might say about you, you will have a difficult time enjoying life.

What are the negative thoughts that go through your head about others and what others think of you?

Others think I am …

Others don't think I can …

Others probably find me …

I think others might be afraid or wary of me because …

Others label me as …

This makes me feel …

Now that you have written these thoughts, take a big heavy black marker and put a big **X** through all of the thoughts above. When these negative thoughts come into your head, picture that big X, reminding you not to worry about what others think.

Erasing the Stigma of Mental Health Issues

Focus on Your Strengths

You can do many things to help fight the stigma associated with your issue. You can focus on your strengths rather than your limitations. Demonstrate to others, and yourself, that you have a great deal to offer.

In the spaces that follow, identify some of your strengths. You have much to share, so take a few minutes to think about and write about some of your greatest strengths.

My strengths related to the community:

_____

_____

My strengths related to relationships with others:

_____

_____

My strengths related to my work or volunteer job:

_____

_____

My strengths related to creativity:

_____

_____

My strengths related to special skills I possess:

_____

_____

How can you share these strengths to show others that despite and/or because of your traumatic event issues, you are a talented human being?

_____

_____

Ways I Try to Minimize My Trauma Stress

Many people dealing with the stress that occurs after a traumatic event will try a variety of ways to minimize its stigma.

Complete the following table to explore the various ways that you minimize your issues and how this makes you feel. Describe some better ways to cope. Use name codes.

Ways I Minimize My Traumatic Event Issues	The Effect This Has on Me and Others	A Better Way to Cope
Example: I pretend that nothing is wrong with me.	*Others think I should just get over it and move on with my life.*	*Explain and say that I've been having some recurring nightmare of my trauma and I'm working to cope.*
I pretend that nothing is wrong with me		
I refuse to get help		
I say things like "Nothing can ever help me"		
I will not talk about my mental health issues		
I laugh and make jokes about my actions		
I avoid people		
Other		

Erasing the Stigma of Mental Health Issues

Ways I Am Treated

Think about some of the ways that people treat you because of the symptoms you show. In the spaces below, explore the various ways people treat you.

Write about those who treat you unfairly and why. Use Name Codes.

I am rejected by family …

[ ]

I am rejected by my friends …

[ ]

I encounter problems at work …

[ ]

I encounter problems at home …

[ ]

I am subjected to physical violence or harassment …

[ ]

I am laughed at …

[ ]

I treat myself unfairly by …

[ ]

I treat myself fairly by …

[ ]

Managing Trauma Workbook for Teens

Self-Doubt

Don't let stigma create self-doubt and shame. One of the most important ways to minimize the stigma of a trauma is to explore how one doubts oneself. Self-doubt almost always stems from a lack of understanding rather than information based on the facts. Feeling ashamed, embarrassed or guilty because of what you experienced can be self-defeating.

How does the stress associated with having lived through a traumatic event cause you to doubt yourself, and how can you control your self-doubt in a positive and strong way?

Ways I Doubt Myself	How This Negatively Affects Me	What I Can Do About it
EXAMPLE: I think that I am somehow responsible and should have been stronger.	I don't ever feel good about myself.	Identify my current strengths and think about how the trauma has made me stronger.

> *However you arrive at the ability to ignore self-doubt - if you can acquire it or possess it or find it or discover it – move beyond self-doubt.*
> ~ Dwight Yoakum

How do you relate to this quotation? _____

_____

_____

Erasing the Stigma of Mental Health Issues

A Poster about the STIGMA of People Who have Experienced a Trauma

In the space that follows, draw a collage of pictures, symbols and/or words, of how you believe you are being stigmatized by others.

A Poster about ACCEPTANCE of People Who have Experienced a Trauma

In the space that follows, create a collage of words from magazines, of what you believe the stress related to a personal trauma is like, when one is accepted.

Erasing the Stigma of Mental Health Issues

DE-STIGMA-TIZE with the Facts about Mental Health Issues

Myth: Mental health issues are rare.
Fact: Mental health issues are not rare and affect nearly everyone either directly or indirectly.

Myth: People with mental health issues are unable to lead successful, productive lives.
Fact: Most people with a mental health issues respond to treatment, learn to cope with and manage their problems, and go on to lead productive and fulfilling lives.

Myth: People who have mental health issues will not get better.
Fact: Once diagnosed, mental health issues are treatable. While they are not always cured, they can be managed effectively. Most people with mental health issues live productive and positive lives. Many receive therapy and medications. Individuals with severe or persistent mental health issues who do not respond well to therapy or meds may require more support, or different therapists or meds, and they do well; and some may not function as highly as others.

Myth: People with mental health problems are violent and unpredictable.
Fact: While some people who suffer from mental health issues do commit antisocial acts, a mental health issue does not equal criminality or violence - despite the media's tendency to emphasize a suspected link. People with mental illness are no more likely to commit violent acts than anyone in the general public, but they are more likely to be victimized and are more likely to inflict violent actions on themselves.

Myth: Mental health issues happen because of bad parenting or personal weakness.
Fact: The main risk factors for mental health issues are not bad parenting or personal weakness but rather genetics, severe and prolonged stress (such as physical or sexual abuse), or other environmental influences (such as birth trauma or head injury).

Myth: Treatments for mental health issues is not usually effective.
Fact: The effectiveness of any treatment depends on a number of factors including the type of mental issue and the particular needs of the individual. A combination of psychiatric medication and psychotherapy, or social interventions are the most effective ways to treat mental health issues.

Myth: Mental health issues are caused by everyday stressors.
Fact: It may seem that stress is responsible for mental health issues; however, there is no one clear cause of mental health issues. Rather, it is a result of complex interactions between psychological, biological, genetic and social factors. Stress, stigma, and lack of support can make it worse for the individual.

Myth: Mental health issues are always hereditary.
Fact: Some mental health issues include a genetic component, which results in a predisposition or vulnerability toward the illness among children and siblings, but environment also plays a key role in the development of certain mental health issues. If someone in one's family has mental health issues, that person will be at higher risk.

If you start to experience the symptoms of a mental health issue, it is important for you to see a medical professional to determine if you have a problem that will require treatment. If you know of anyone who seems to have symptoms of a mental health issue, urge that person to do the same.

Coping with the Stigma of a Mental Health Issue

Get treatment. Don't let the fear of being labeled with a mental health issue prevent you from seeking help. Treatment can provide relief by identifying and reducing symptoms that interfere with your school work and personal life. How can you arrange treatment? _____

_____

_____

_____

Don't let stigma create self-doubt and shame. If you are buying into the stigma, you will have the mistaken belief that your issue is a sign of personal weakness, or that you should be able to control it better. How can you have less self-doubt? _____

_____

_____

_____

How can you have less shame? _____

_____

_____

_____

Don't isolate yourself. Have the courage to confide in your family members, friends, partner, clergy, therapist, or other members of your community. Who can you reach out to and who can you trust for the compassion, support and understanding you need? _____

_____

_____

_____

Get help at work. If you are having unwanted stress after experiencing a trauma and it is affecting your work, confidentially talk with your supervisor, explain what you are doing to help yourself, and find out what plans and programs are available that might help. _____

_____

_____

_____

If you and others are willing, share responses.

Erasing the Stigma of Mental Health Issues

Speak Out Against Stigmas

Speaking out can help instill courage in others who are facing trauma issues, and it will help to educate the public about the effect that these issues have on you personally. Speaking out for and about yourself advocates for others who might have these issues and it can be beneficial to you at the same time.

Think about ways that you might let your voice be heard about stigmas and their damaging effects on people. For each of the items, list the ways that you could speak out against stigmas.

Express your opinions at events. What events are planned in your place of employment where you might speak out against stigmas? _____
_____
_____

At what events in your community might you volunteer to speak out against stigmas? _____
_____
_____

You could write an informative feature article or letter to the editor of a local newspaper or magazine. What would you say? _____
_____
_____

You could blog about stigmas on the Internet. How can you do this? _____
_____
_____

What are some other ways to speak out against stigmas? _____
_____
_____

How do you think speaking out will benefit others? _____
_____
_____

How will it benefit you? _____
_____
_____

Whole Person Associates is the leading publisher of training resources for professionals who empower people to create and maintain healthy lifestyles. Our creative resources will help you work effectively with your clients in the areas of stress management, wellness promotion, mental health and life skills.

Please visit us at our web site: **www.wholeperson.com**. You can check out our entire line of products, place an order, request our print catalog, and sign up for our monthly special notifications.

Whole Person Associates
800-247-6789